REFLECTIONS, LOVE UNTIL DEATH

By Huang Mei

TESTIMONIALS

From China:

'When in spring the silkworms approach death, they spin with the greatest effort; when a candle burns down, tears dry. 'This is the pursuit until death, an inextinguishable love in the heart. The unremitting pursuit of her career, the limitless love for her lovers, her deep feelings for her child, all of this Huang Mei has achieved with her life as the price. Faced with fate, she became riddled with scars but she did not shrink back in the slightest. She took the heavy weight of fate onto her weak shoulders and continued her difficult way, step by step, and finally she achieved the goal and ideal of her love. She has moved us very much. A simple woman who shows inspiring strength, the glow of motherly love, and the determination of a poet.

Yi Ying, professor at the China Central Academy of Fine Arts, famous art critic for contemporary art

In our youth, we were fellow students at Peking University for four years. Huang Mei was always passionate and with a free spirit, and loved to whirl about. After her graduation, she selected the subject aesthetics. I went on to study economics. Today she has become an international ambassador for the arts, and I have become a university professor. In different fields, we both strive for beauty – the beauty of the human soul. Huang Mei's path shows us once more that life isn't made beautiful by the end results but by its journey: holding onto your dream and your love.

Xinzhong Xu, Professor at Guanghua School of Management, Peking University

Reflections, Love until Death, Like a wonderful promise it invites us to dive into Huang Mei's retelling of her experiences: Her feelings and her love, courage and self-confidence, struggle and doubts are all unusual, but after she faced the question about life or death, and was reborn as if from fire, there still remained the lovable and admirable Huang Mei who gives life back its colour.

Life is indeed fragile, many people also think that fate is unavoidable. However, Huang Mei's experiences tell us: One cannot choose one's birth and death but one can decide how to love, how to live, and choose which form one gives to one's life!

Eastern tradition flowing through her veins, Huang Mei is an independent woman who can embrace the spirit humanity's cultures with both arms. She deeply loves her family, nature and art... Love forms a strong soul, it is the power to conquer death. Through her victory, Huang Mei once again recognised the value of life and gained a deeper appreciation for it, and her love became wider and deeper. The extraordinary result is the Huang Mei we see today, full of passion for life. Her story is also a revelation of life.

(He Yunlan: artist, art educationalist, chair of the Women's Art Association Beijing)

From Italy:

Huang Mei's book talks about the great strength of an independent woman in a very intense and comprehensible manner. She faced two of the biggest challenges that life has to offer: disease and the responsibility of motherhood.

Paola Del Vescovo, artist and professor at the Accademia di Belle Arti di Napo

From France:

Huang Mei is not hiding any more. She shares her raw pain and her love for life with her readers. At her side, we sail off across an unquiet and unknown sea. We row between inner darkness and the wonderful discovery of art.

Juliette Montier, artist from France

From Greece:

Living in another country, getting cancer and beating it, getting through the process of divorce and raising a child is not easy!

Amongst other functions, art also always has the function of trauma recovery.

Mei's literature gave her the second life she desperately needed, filled with the positive energy to continue it, filled with meaning.

Floros Floridis, one of the founders of free jazz in Greece and interdisciplinary artist

From Switzerland:

We know Mei as an extraordinary personality, always surrounded by an aura of elegance and with a great sensitivity for art, for which her passion and sparkling intelligence allow her to give other people an understanding. In this book, one learns about her eventful life story that captivates and touches in equal measures, and that gives hope that even the worst blows of fate can be overcome.

Pi-Chin Chien (cellist) & Fabian Müller (composer)

From Germany:

In colourful and poetic images the author describes the stations of her journey, the way from victimhood to an active, imaginative life. The book helps to understand that the strength to survive is within us, and that art can be one of the answers to the complex questions of existence.

Mei Huang's strength and will to live is an example of female, true emancipation.

Jeanine Meerapfel, filmmaker

A deeply touching book that shows us how vulnerable we are, both in body and in mind. However, it also shows how strong we can be when we fight. It has a special value through its authenticity. It demands an attentive reader to recognise its depth. It is not an ordinary book.

Dieter and Margret, married dance partners from Berlin, researchers at a German science institution

Mei, with the image of life as a river, that with its perpetual motion continually brings changes, with the new choices to embrace or to simply accept. Your book has touched me deeply. What a great strength that leads you unwavering to new realisations about freedom.

"In all beginnings dwells a magic force, for guarding us and helping us to live."
{H. Hesse; translation by Richard and Clara Winston}

Sonja Merz, conductor of the Accordian Orchestra Euphonia

An eventful biography of a woman with a strong soul and love for music, who does not give in to destiny.

Just at the beginning of her career she receives a blow of fate that would bring the strongest to their knees; stage-four cancer!
A book that allows an unusually deep look into the soul of Mei Huang, a woman whom I admire. Many people of all ages owe wonderful and formative experiences to her open-mindedness, inventiveness and creativity. I count myself lucky that our paths crossed.

Hedy Stark-Fussnegger: Vice president of the German Accordion Association

From Australia;

Irrespective of the language, Mei's words touch us all. As will her fortitude. This brave and creative woman has a great capacity to understand human nature and place it in words on a page, from which we can all grow.

Pat Grayson, author of 9 books.

Published in Australia
(formally, Love Until Death)
(April 2020 Heart Space Publications
PO Box 1085, Daylesford, Victoria, 3460, Australia,
Tel +61 450260348
www.heartspacepublications.com
pat@heartspacepublication.com
Copyright © Original Title: 向死而爱
Text and images by: Huang Mei
Copyright© Sichuan Tiandi Publishing House CO., LTD, 2018

This edition is published by arrangement with Heart Space Publications.

All rights reserved under international copyright conventions. No part of this book may be reproduced, stored in a retrieval system, or transmitted in any form or by any means electronic, mechanical, photocopying, recorded or otherwise without written permission from Heartspace Publications.

Whilst every care has been taken to check the accuracy of the information in this book, the publisher cannot be held responsible for any errors, omissions or originality.

ISBN 978-0-6486524-0-3

English translation by Zhao Xiang - - 向昭 (Sydney, Australia)

AUSTRALIAN PUBLISHER'S NOTE

Mei's story is not lineal, where she travels into the distant past, to the recent past, and into the current moment. Nevertheless, she wrote mostly in the present tense (of that time), as if a diary entry. At times, when talking about the past, it is still written in the present tense. Within a paragraph, she refers to the past, but still in the present tense. We have kept to her method to honor her emotive and insightful state by doing so. However, some may find this a bit uneasy to start with, but we ask you to continue as it will be worth the effort.

In places, the writing may seem stilted. We tried to retain the text as if Mei was speaking, knowing that English is not her first language.

Illustrations

All the illustrations are created by Ms. Qu Yin, crafted from photos provided by Huang Mei.

CONTENTS

Cancer	1
I Thought You Would Die	5
Create Life	13
You are Crazy	23
Doctor Tony	33
Irrevocable Break-up	45
I Hate My Body	53
Return to Work With Pain of Body	57
Social Dancing in Berlin	65
Hendrik	67
Movement under the waist	81
I keep away from Hendrik	87
World Culture Palace of Berlin, 20th July 2003 Night	95
I Want Go Back To China	97
Piano And Love	101
Stephan	107
JIM	113
Green Wedding	127
Frustration, Cultural Clash	137
Jim's precarious job position	145
The night that changed my life	155
Divorced	159
Jim	169
What Is Living? How To Be Alive?	177
Jim and Tantan	183

Bogelt	185
Lake Constance	191
A Year End Phone Call	197
The Diary	203
A Little Rabbit Looks for Mum	207
Light Festival In Kindergarten	209
Is Life Heavy?	213
I carry on	215
Postscript:	217
Look for Hope in Despair	217

CANCER

Cancer... yes, cancer. And I'm a single mum – so life has really started for me. Or is it about to end?

That was many years ago, and after all I have gone through I decided to write these reflections. It was December, the year 2000. It did not matter if it was the beginning of a new year or the end of the old one, people were 'ringing in the new century'. I was in Germany, as an overseas student. I went to Beijing University when only sixteen years old to do a BA. At twenty, I was a student of Zehou Li, a famous professor of Chinese History and Culture. This was to pursue my Master's degree in Art. I was the first Chinese student who was recognised by the German Education Department at that time, to study for my doctorate. In time, I gained it with a high distinction.

With Mr. and Mrs. Li Zehou

Things happened quickly, for soon thereafter I gave birth to a chubby, cutie of a son (Tantan). In that year of 2000, Germany hosted the World Trade Fair in Hanover. Actually, it was The First Lady of Germany who offered me a specialist job at the Fair. I was thirty-six years old; my year of fate.

My token animal in China is the dragon. The dragon represents wisdom, fortitude, and strength of character. Not bad traits, if they come to the fore. I would need them in the times to come. For me, the new century was scary and exciting at the same time. I worked long and hard, and with good endeavour for the year. I was rewarded with buckets of money, for my son and me.

However, at the end of the year, a bolt out of the blue changed everything. As a birthday present I received a diagnosis of stage four rectal cancer, that had metastasised – I had little tumours invading the liver, and it was in the lymph.

Happy birthday Mei.

Too young! The doctors lamented.

In order to save my young life, on 18th December, before Christmas, the doctors operated. Massive incisions were made to remove the tumours and rectum, as both proved to be malignant.

China allows relatives to sleep at the hospital of a loved one; I needed that. Hospitals in Germany do not allow this.

After the surgery, the bleeding did not stop. My attending doctor could not hide his concern and asked the nurse to notify my relatives – this was ominous. The nurse said that she had already asked when I was registered; I had no other relatives in Germany apart from my one-year-old son.

I slipped into a coma, as if on a boat, floating with the tide. The white god of death stood silently at the bow and let the boat drift towards the end. Clouds rolled across the sky, and waves crashed on the shoreline, all hastening me.

It was an odd feeling, floating as I did, when I wanted to live. Desperately wanted to live. I had my little boy… I had me. Life had only just begun. The glare of the dark night made me scream and scream, all within the coma.

I screamed, the boat should sail to a safe shore... On a cliff, there should be a tree of life... In the illusion of the coma, I struggled to move my body, to fight on, but in reality, I could neither move, nor speak.

Finally, like a cork, slowly drifting to the shore, I landed. When I opened my eyes my first sensation was that my arms were cold... then I saw Jim. He stood in front of the bed holding a bunch of flowers. But this person, my ex-husband, or perhaps a friend – he was no longer my relative. He did not even give me a child.

Embarrassed, and feeling somewhat ashamed of my helplessness, I smiled but turned my head aside to avoid Jim seeing my tears. I would have turned my entire body away from him but my arms were full of tubes and needles. I could not stop the flood of tears.

In my silent tears, I heard Jim crying. His voice when he spoke was hesitant, stopping and starting, "Mei, Mei... you woke up... I thought you would die..."

Hearing this, my entire body stiffened. Every nerve, every cell became alert, like a small rodent when the fox looms above. Gone was the shame. I turned my head back to face him to see what folly he was saying. Now I did not care if he saw my tears.

"I feel ashamed as you call me Mei, in the same way as if we were still married and in love. Sometimes you say stupid things... how could I die, how can I die? Tantan is still so little". I looked up to see Jim, I couldn't talk anymore and closed my eyes weakly.

I THOUGHT YOU WOULD DIE

Lying on the hospital bed, I blame and hate my fate. Why me? Why me, who is so young to have this cancer? After all these years Jim's visit upsets me. He thought I would die. I close my eyes, but Jim is calling me, in all different tones of "Mei", reverberates in my brain.

I had told Jim the story of how I got my name. I was born in winter. On the day when my mum birthed me, the plum tree outside the window bloomed. So my dad named me "Mei", which is the Chinese word for 'plum flower'.

My mother's second child was also a girl. With the third pregnancy, the doctor told her that it's a boy, and persuaded her to keep it. However, my parents decided to abort him as they wanted to put all their effort into their two daughters (at that stage China had not introduced the 'one child policy'). Seemingly though, since then my parents started to treat me, their first daughter, more like a boy than a girl. My father took every opportunity to strengthen me, "Mei, born as the flower, not afraid of the coldness of winter… that your whole life blooms like the plum flower, without fear, or difficulty, standing proudly against the snow".

Jim was my boyfriend, who became my husband. After hearing this story he fell in love with plum flowers. When he called me, he always raised the inflection in his voice, "Mei-plum flower". When upset, his tone would change to the fourth German tone of Mei, as if addressing a younger sister. Or, he called in a mixed-chaos, "Mei – Plum, Mei… Younger Sister, Mei… Younger Sister, Mei-Plum". These changes in modulation sometimes made me happy and sometimes annoyed me.

Closing my eyes, I thought, when people are dying, they always say kind words. Because my words were not kind at the time, I still shouted at Jim with anger. Usually, my anger was well hidden in the deepest crevice of my being, and Jim could not tell.

6 | Reflections, love until death

One night in a pub, Jim walked went straight to the unattended music stand. On one knee he played the piano. I was mesmerised with his long fingers as they expertly quickly under the soft light. It was in that moment that I knew I wanted to marry him.

When I was a kid, I suffered from many diseases. I had pleurisy at three years of age, pneumonia at four. When these were cleared, at five I got hepatitis. Hepatitis is not so easily cured, consequently it constantly relapsed. Until I was about fifteen my liver was swollen. Of course my mum, in a way, blamed me and kept saying, "Why don't you get meningitis?" (The Chinese term for Meningitis is 'Nao Mo Yan', where 'Yan' means inflammation, but also salt.) "I would rather you get 'Nao Mo Yan' and be a bit stupid, than the other 'Yans', which put your body at great risk." She would half joke and half scold, "I'd prefer you to save the other 'Yan' for me to cook with, then I can have less worry and save my energy".

When I was little, I was very weak. Mum took me to hospital frequently. I was smart, and always ranked first place in both primary and middle school. However, Mum never thought this was a great achievement; she showed little interest in my academic achievements. Instead, she meticulously kept all my medical records – she hoped that I would avoid being sent to the rural areas to spent time as a farm labourer. This was one of Chairman Mao's policies. My ill health was worth it, if I could avoid this.

In 1977, China started a drive to educate through universities. This was at the time I graduated from high school, and I was determined to attend university. For the admission process, Mum panicked and burnt my medical records as she was afraid that her daughter would not pass the health check. She thought that by destroying the files she could pretend that her daughter had never suffered any malady.

This was all a waste, as by that time my health issues had settled and I passed the medical exam on the first attempt – I was accepted by Beijing University. My mother, though, could not let go and would say, "You suffered enough disease, now you should have acquired enough immunity for the rest of your life".

The years passed, and I happily graduated with distinctions and continued on to pursue my Master's degree. After this graduation, I went to Germany to do my doctorate, which I previously explained.

Now, at thirty-six, with my son just having turned one, I cry about having cancer, and shout, "I hate you cancer, hate, hate".

Laying in the hospital with all kinds of tubes, lines, electrodes, and drips, all giving and taking from my body, I lay there in a kind of stupor and cannot get Jim's words out of my head, "I thought you would die". They sting, like angry hornets. *Doesn't Jim know how anxious I already am?* I am so fearful. That diagnosis scares the hell out of me.

As time went on, I was released from hospital, but I was constantly back having one test or another. Its affliction became ever clearer, and as it did, the pressure on me increased. One day, when having a scan of my liver and heart, I was naked, standing in the dark, behind the machine, being told to do this and that. My heartbeat so thunderous, like a herd of wild horses pounding within my heart cavity. When younger, during my healthy period, I remembered having photos taken when I was naked and sunning in the warm sunshine... nature is a nice thing. But at that moment, being exposed and scanned under the civil modality made me feel indignant, frustrated, helpless and hopeless.

Hooray. After the doctor checked the images he told me that there was no sign of cancer in my liver or chest. As if he was the saviour, I kept thanking him. However, not so fast. I was not in safe territory. Two days later I had a CT scan on the abdomen area, liver and chest. My fears worsened, like a punch in the stomach. It was announced that my liver had many small tumours. The surgeon felt that they could cut it out through the rectum. This did not seem realistic to me, as they had told me that I was stage four cancer and that there were many tumours, so how could they get them all? When they told me it had spread into the lymph, I was crushed, as if an avalanche of a thousand rocks had fallen upon me.

The days before the surgery I sat in front of my computer and researched everything I could about stomach anatomy – what is the large intestine, small intestine, rectum, duodenum? What is cancer, first stage, stage two, stage three, and what does stage four mean to me? Stage four is the worst stage there is. I learnt about metastasis, and could understand that my cancer had metastasised to the liver. What is radiotherapy, chemotherapy, etc.? I gave myself enough knowledge to petrify myself, but not enough to see any hope.

Another thing, the doctor said the location of the cancer is very unlucky. I'm unlucky to have cancer in the first place. This bad luck worsened because the cancer was only seven to eight centimetres from my anus – my anus had to be removed! This blow was even harder to take than accepting the cancer.

I was in Germany, and so I rang hospitals all over China; Beijing, Shanghai, Guangzhou, etc. to make enquires, seeking a bit of hope.

"Come", some said, "come to our hospital. We can do the surgery without removing the anus. But even if we do, we can give you another one. Come back to China and come to our hospital, we have enough experience and the price is cheaper".

I'm terrified, and constantly open my hands and ask for help. But in the end, I place my empty hands in my lap. I have a year old son here in Germany.

My son is my only relative here. Before the surgery, I went to see my Chief Surgeon, but he was not there. A young doctor saw me. I pleaded with this young doctor not to remove my anus. I also wanted to know: even though my liver was riddled with cancer, what if they cannot get all the cancer out of my liver? What happens then?

The doctor, clearly uncomfortable, tried to comfort me by saying, "You are so young, believe me. We will try every possible method to keep your anus intact. If we do not get all the cancer, we have other ways, such as chemotherapy, which can be successful in removing those small tumours".

The doctor had relaxed a bit and his voice calmer, which helped me settle. I felt more comfortable.

The night before the surgery, I went to the cinema with Yun, my Chinese boyfriend, and watched a movie. After I was diagnosed with cancer, I continuously bled in my stools, and I lost a lot of weight. A photo was taken. I was slim, and thought I looked nice.

At that time, even with the bad news and prospects, I was scared, but never thought I would die. Perhaps I did not allow myself to think that way, but I did remain hopeful. If I thought I would die, how could I sit in the cinema and watch the chick flick?

In China, people would not be so insensitive to blurt out "I thought you would die". Jim said it straight out. When I married him, I was not so young, almost thirty. I felt more mature than him but thought Jim was the right person for me. Yet, it still ended in divorce. I knew that it would be me who would feel the disappointment for the rest of my life. And if this cancer ultimately claims me, I will regret that we divorced. He had no right to say what he did. He was funny like that, perhaps being German he saw things in a different way. For instance, he would not allow me to call my mother-in-law 'Mum'. He said that his mum had four children already, too many. It would be too funny if I called her Mum as well. Another example was when we talked about having a child after we married; he was afraid that our child's eyes would be slanted. He thought this would be funny, but this funny hurt. Always such silly words from him.

This is one of the reasons why we divorced. Yet, Jim loved me very much. Did I have to divorce him? No. I was very sick. I forgave him, and I hate myself so much. Jim is not my husband anymore. Nor is he now my relative. But he came to visit me with a bunch of flowers after my surgery. His tears woke me from my coma. The first sentence he said still made me upset. I was angry and I didn't want to open my eyes to see him. I hear Jim's voice again, "Mei, you are the plum flower. Now the plum flower is going to bloom. You are always so strong. You must get better soon. You are right, you have Tantan, your son. He is so young, he needs his mum, he needs you. You like flowers. You see, I brought these plum flowers for you. You know I have not bought flowers for a long time". Of course, I did know that, "I bought them because you are here. These are a new species of flowers from the florist... I will buy them for you. There are books too. You like to read, but you cannot read now... Next time when I come to see you, I will bring more books for you. You will be strong again after reading".

Yes, my son, flowers and books. After I heard Jim's words, I had a stronger desire to return to my life – the warmth passed over my whole body. I felt that this warmth was the start of my recovery. Without me, Jim would not need to buy flowers, why would he say this. Yet, what he said made me feel better. I was embarrassed. I wish Jim would have said that he would play the piano for me. But Jim did not say this. Actually, Jim never said he would play the piano for me. There were a few men in my life who said they would play the piano for me, but they never did. The romantic feelings are just an illusion. It was Jim, who for a few years played the piano – his performance melted into my blood. But Jim never said that he would play the piano for me, he played for himself. The first thing I did after I divorced Jim was to buy a piano, even though I can only play a few simple songs. The important thing is that there is a piano standing, waiting.

Jim left. I could imagine his mourning if I did not open my eyes. Jim is 185 centimetres tall. He's like one of Alberto Giacometti's statues. I am only 160 centimetres high. I felt he was too high to reach to up to. When he was down in the dumps, Jim's shoulder slouched to a low position. His whole back lost its shape. The one who was a prince in my eyes would become ugly. I know that if I died Jim would fail to rouse himself, his shoulders would drop, and his back would become rounded. He would be ugly. I could imagine this even without opening my eyes. I was prepared to hold Jim with my strength, to uplift him forever, and encourage him to be his best. That feeling was really good, but I did not make it. We divorced.

CREATE LIFE

Our marriage did not survive, mainly because of our cultural differences. The economic crisis in Germany did not help.

When younger, and rushing at everything, as young people seem to do, I descended into Yun's love web. Women, when in love, often find excuses to justify things, and to their behaviour. I am the same. I decided to make a baby with Yun. In this way, 'I will take a knife to cut off the water' (this is an old Chinese saying, and in Mei's case showed her determination to divorce Jim, and have a baby with Yun, irrespective of the consequences). I made the decision on 25th September 1998. It was a Friday, the last two days before the German national Election Day. In the last election campaign of the German Social Democratic Party, I was full of passion. I wanted to break up with Jim and his German culture, to forge my own path. I wanted to have a baby with this Chinese man, Yun. Even though this Chinese man had nothing, no finances, or prospects.

During my pregnancy, I wrote in my diary, and was frank to my child to be; "My child, when you were just four or five days conceived, Mum has already felt you. Mum's stomach feels sick, but there is an amazing feeling around my lower abdomen. Mum is wondering, is this the process of a shaping life, or one that was passing over?

A few days later a doctor confirmed your existence. You didn't disappoint Mum's stubborn wish. I turned thirty-four. Can you imagine? To create you, your father gave his seed and genealogy. I have great delight to welcome you, to be your mum. Your father and mother believe that we can make your very being in just one time. For this day of creation, your father travelled 600km by train to meet me – from Berlin to Frankfurt, then to Bonn. You are the result of life's miracle. On the day we made you, your mother and father were still in a fit of pique. We fought. In this diary, I will record everything honestly. When you grow up and learn of this, you may laugh, or you may learn about life from it.

Mum and dad were lovers who fell in love, crazily. We made a decision to create your life. We met in a hotel. We dined together. In order to celebrate the coming of you, I ordered a bottle of French wine. However, we fought over who would pay for this bottle of wine. Your dad was a poor student who had to work part-time while he studied for his degree. He knew that my income is higher than his, because at that time, I had completed my Ph.D. in art education, and had a well-paying job. He thought that Mummy's ordering of this bottle of wine was too much of a luxury, and that I should pay. I thought that as a lady, and carrying his child, he as the man should be gallant enough to pay. After all, shouldn't the mother-to-be be spoiled?

The French wine was warm and spicy; after drinking it, your father got over his annoyance and became excited. I was annoyed, as in my culture the man should always pay for their girlfriend, and he is of my culture.

Even more, the following night, your father went to see another woman. Although they were supposed to only be work-related friends. I was upset. During that period, Mum worked hard to build up a financial base for your arrival. I accumulated all the funds necessary to welcome you. You see child, when I knew you were coming I decided to resign from work and stay at home to give you a good full-time prenatal education. I did this because the best teacher for a child is their mother.

In those special days, Mum hoped that your father would help me through the pregnancy, and join in our excitement of your coming. It seems that your father didn't realise how important it was, like your mum did. He didn't seem to think of his soon to-be-born as a miracle. He went to see that other woman. Although they are just work-related friends, Mum felt wronged… I felt let down. If you were a boy, what would you think and do? You see, when, during the time of making you, Mum and Dad didn't get along, the only thing that we cannot give up is you".

Many years later, when I looked through my diary of that time, I recognised the hand of fate. Actually, the me at that time spent many years with Jim, and Jim's family, living a good middle to upper class life.

When I fell in love with Yun, I could not change my desire for the upper middle class of living. The same, I could not get used to being with a poor student, Yun. Conversely, Yun couldn't immediately adapt to my lifestyle.

Time passed quickly, and we continued to argue. In July 1999, Tantan was born. It did not take long before my savings were almost used up. After staying at home and breastfeeding him for three months, I had to return to work. By doing so, I got on with life and the need to earn money.

Actually, when Tantan was born, my culture prefers us women to rest for a month. But I felt ready. The first thing I did was to send a letter to the responsible person who looked after foreign affairs for the City Council of Berlin. I wrote to enquire if there were Chinese and German culture exchange projects for which I could offer my services. The responsible person welcomed my letter and invited me to attend an interview. He wanted me to work on the youth project for the German World Expo.

In 2000, through the German World Expo, Yun and I worked together on this and made a lot of money. Yun dreamed of making more money. He registered a company in China and used our money to open a luxurious office in China, and to build his career. I remained in Germany to stand on my own two feet, whether I wanted to or not. Tantan was over one year old and so cute, things looked promising.

In 2000, I took care of my son whilst working as well. There was no time for social or rest related activities but I was satisfied. At the end of the year, after the end of the German World Expo, I started haemorrhaging. I called Yun to ask him come back to Germany. He was preparing to celebrate Christmas with his friends when I called. His first reaction when he heard the news that I was sick, and to have serious surgery, was not good, saying, "… that you always overreact, and pay too much attention to yourself… and isn't this just cancer… you'll be okay, won't you?" I nagged, and reluctantly he returned to Germany.

After Yun and I went to the cinema, the day before the operation, he took me home and we made love. It was good, it was exciting, but there was pain. The tumour in my rectal area was irritated and blood dyed the bedsheet.

Vaguely, I remember the time when I had my first period. It stained my white school uniform, soaked the wooden stool, and dripped blood onto the classroom floor. I nearly died of embarrassment. From then on, I had the feeling that females were inferior to males.

I hoped that I would fall in love with a man who would protect and support me, no matter what. Yun's caustic comments would cut deeper than the surgeon's knife on the following day. His immaturity and ego-driven way emerged more than ever.

Oh sunshine in the sky, so brilliant and vibrant. Oh men ploughing the fields, and women weaving, hundreds of children playing. Tantan, only one year old. He's so lovely, but I feel he is lonely. I want to give him a sister, and give birth to this sister with Yun. The relationship between Yun and I is not good any more, although I still hope. I want Tantan to have a sister who shares the same father and mother. I very much want to be alive. I want another child. In my desire, I shout, "I want to live". The nuclear bomb in my heart exploded and gave off a mushroom cloud that encompassed all of my being. I fell into a deep sleep.

The next day, when I woke up, I reached a turning point in my life. I am stage four cancer, is it too late for me? I was pushed into the surgery.

The Christmas of 1999 was Tantan's first Christmas. I was busy until the afternoon of Christmas Eve before I had time to do Christmas shopping. It was nearly closing time. Other than a few late shoppers, like myself, most people were back home. I bought a Christmas tree for half price. It was dark when I got home. I turned on the cluster of silver Christmas lights, and held Tantan whilst I decorated the tree. I then played the piano and sang carols to my son, '*Silent night, Holy night, Shepherds' quake at the sight. Glories stream from heaven afar, Christ the Saviour is born, Christ the Saviour is born. Holy night Son of God love's pure light Radiant beams from Thy holy face with the dawn of redeeming grace Jesus Lord at Thy birth Jesus Lord at Thy birth Silent night, holy night All is dark, save the light Yonder, where the sweet vigils keep O'er the Babe, who in silent sleep Rests in heavenly peace Rests in heavenly peace Amen*'.

In 2000, I am unable to buy a Christmas tree for my son. I am unable to decorate the Christmas tree with my son. As his mother, my dedication to him could not be stronger. On the morning of the surgery

I took the navy blue diary, which recorded all Tantan's growth with me to hospital. When I arrived, I longed to see a photo of Tantan. I asked Yun to choose one for me and bring it to hospital. Yun took Tantan to a day care centre, then came to the hospital with the photo.

I was lying on the white sheeted surgery bed with a white sheet over my body. A nurse pushed me into the operating theatre. When my son's photo was placed in my hand, the operating theatre door closed. Later, Yun told me that during the operation he went out to do something more important. I knew that the operation was to take about six hours, and was not expecting anyone to wait all that time, but I had hoped he would. My only companions were my son's photo and that navy blue diary.

To me, this is my fate.

Christmas morning of 2000, I lay quietly on the white bed.

I had been active for thirty-six years, then suddenly sick, perhaps dying. No matter how hard I try, I cannot move. I have never been like this before.

Under the anaesthetic I do not know how much time passed. In my dream, the room started to shake. The pictures that hung on the wall were no longer flowers or fruit. They became newly born babies. Some babies held up by their fathers' hands, the naughty sleeping baby who holds a toy beetle; babies lying among flowers all smiling sweetly... I felt that the ward I stayed in with Mrs. Web (in the other bed) disappeared, all the antibiotics and drip bottles of pain killers, all disappeared... The ward became Tantan's room, navy blue bed, sky blue lights. I thought I was having him all over again...multi-coloured-balls, mostly blue, lake blue and aquatic tubs...... from which he was born. He cried loudly, and the whole world smiled. The flowers are happy, Mother smiles, my parents came from China, I feel proud. Flowers from friends fill the delivery room... ah ah, this is not my ward, it's my son's delivery room, I almost shout out.

25th December 2000, Christmas Day I spent by myself. A day of sadness and confusion. I do not understand why that night God took away the elderly lady in the bed opposite mine. God should deliver children like Tantan here.

Are there really boundaries between life and death?

I remembered the boxwood trees with small leaves, which grow in the northern area of China. There the winters are dry and cold. Sometimes leaves from young trees dry yellow, some even dry to a whitish colour. I thought of these leaves dying and falling to the ground. But by the next spring, these leaves will gradually become green. I observed the whole process carefully over that long period, and when the green covered dried leaves, it was really nature's miracle. Life's miracle. These two words obsessed me for that entire Christmas day.

26th December, my parents came from China to Germany, tears hung in my mum's eyes. Tantan's clothes, from his shirt to jeans, to his little shoes on his feet, are all famous Italian brands that I had bought for him. When he was born, his father bought an outfit for him from Italy when he was there for business. I once lent this outfit to a girlfriend for her son when he was born. I warned my friend to return it to me when the child grew out of it. Which she did. I kept my son's famous clothing brand. Later though, I changed my value system, and chose not to buy famous brands for him anymore. At that same time I spent less time and money on my own appearance, and more on Tantan's. Whenever I went out shopping, I always went to kids stores hunting for children's clothes, shoes, etc. I had outfits of different colour, and different styles for every day. I, in turn, didn't care about myself.

Now, with my parents he comes to visit me. Seeing me he runs to me. He is so adorable. He does not understand the difference between home and hospital. He does not know that his mother is close to death. He has not seen me for over ten days, he runs towards his mum's hug. He does not see the needles in my arm. Nor can he see the wounds that wracked me with pain. Fortunately, a nurse intercepts him and slows him down. He is right in front of me and I feel sad because I am unable to hug my son.

I notice eczema on his skin. It has flared up and roughened because I have not been there to rub cream on him. There are two rashes on his white face, like two patches on white cloth. My eyes sting. I am unable to stop the tears, and whimper. The nurse is confused, and touches my shoulder and says, "Oh, Ms. Mei, you are very strong. Since you have been in this hospital, you're always optimistic... All the doctors praise you. But now your son comes, such a lovely little boy... so why are you crying?"

I am unable to answer. Seldom do I cry for myself or my life. But I often cry for friends' stories. Or sometimes I cry in a cinema, I cry when I read, and always need lots of tissues. Now I am crying for my son, should I answer why?

Maybe it is more than that. I am crying because I have just had major surgery for stage four cancer. There are needles all over my hands and arms, I have several drips feeding into me. I should be stronger in front of my parents, and the nurse, but seeing my son opened the emotion.

German hospitals also do not allow very long visiting time. My parents, also tearful, had to take Tantan home. I went back to my bed, a white ward, white guardrail and white bed sheets. Out of the window, the green pine towers were covered in white snow. Even the floor is white.

I am catapulted from the warm atmosphere of my son's visit, his laughing voice, even his screaming, to the coldness of the hospital. As he is taken his screams fill the corridor. Now that he has gone, the corridor becomes quiet again. The silence is cold and terrifies the patients. They feel helpless despair. In this ward, most of the patients are cancer patients. Most of them are elderly. This is an unhappy ward. There are no new births, new life crying, and full of flowers.

Thinking these things I cannot stop my tears. Tantan is too young. He has eczema. He is as little as a baby tree, and cannot have no mother. Then it hits me. If I die, Tartan is unlikely to remember me.

Pregnant for ten months, struggled with the delivery, Cesarean cut scar, breastfeeding day and night. We recently started to play hide and seek, of course reading picture-books, we listened to music together…, I'm indescribably disconsolate.

The me before that Christmas, and me after that Christmas are vastly different. I clearly knew that somehow I have to walk out of this ward, for my son, for myself.

After Christmas Yun wanted to go back to Beijing. The thought was unbearable. He called the hospital and said he did not have the time to come and say goodbye to me. At that time I was lying on the bed, a needle in my neck having an infusion. I do not remember the excuse that I gave the nurse to stop the infusion, but she did. I wrapped myself in a dressing gown and hobbled downstairs. It was the eighth day after my surgery, and the fifth day of being transferred out of ICU. It was a cold, windy, and snow-filled day. Every step an agony of a thousand knives. Teeth gritted, I headed towards the front door, then to the gates of the hospital. I could hardly raise my arm to wave for the taxi that was parked in a rank a hundred metres down the road. I even took off my scarf to wave. The driver ignored me. I moved three small steps for what would normally be one step. I had to stop and rest. The hundred metres was my target. I proceeded, at snail pace. After getting into the taxi, the driver apologised, "I'm sorry. I saw you but you looked like a drunken or crazy person. I didn't dare to pick you up." I did not blame him. I thought he probably did not notice my waving as it is normal that German taxi drivers read inside of their cars.

I was shocked at what he said. Am I like a drunk? Am I like a crazy person? Are these true? Nevertheless, I just want to see my Yun before he leaves our home... how could he leave and not want come to the hospital to say goodbye?

As soon as I entered my house the phone rang. It was the nurse on duty at the hospital "Ms. Mei, are you home? Thank goodness... you must return immediately to the hospital. We are responsible for you, and we are liable by law". Normally, this nurse is nice, but now she was determined. She agreed that I could stay at home for ten minutes. Yun was packing, slowly, he had not gone. It was not like he had no time. I touched my son while I waited for the taxi.

The nurse in charge burst in as soon as I was resettled. With a stern look said, "Ms. Mei, you may have a doctor's degree, but it is not medicine. Don't you understand, you have a drip connected to your artery, if there was an accident on the road, you would haemorrhage, and be dead in a few minutes... Your son is cute, that I know, but he could lose his mother, forever. I will also lose my job because of this. I have two kids, and my kids would have no food to eat due to me not earning a living".

My tears rolled. In order to see Yun, I took such a risk, and with drip attachments still in my neck. I am not afraid to die, but must live for my son. These tears are for all the anguish I suffer, and now with this castigation, I feel sorry for this young nurse. I wiped away my tears, her words brought to my mind my responsibility to Tantan, and also for myself. I need to conserve my energy for that responsibility.

YOU ARE CRAZY

After the surgery, my body will never seem the same. I have no rectum, I lost my anus, I lost my sphincter. I now have hoses and pipes, attached to buckets and bottles. My body, once a shrine, now a mess. Later I know that I will desire love, desire sex, but I am full of fear, afraid of pain, afraid that I cannot make love anymore, because my body is missing parts, different, horrible. This cannot be my body, this perverted thing. Yet, inside, I feel the same. It seems a century passed since the day before my surgery when Yun and I made love.

Several months later Yun returned to face my sick and horrible body. He is gentle and patient. The doctors are hopeful of recovery. I may live. I have been given a chance to continue my deep passion for Yun. I would like to be repaired; without pain, no barriers, to return back to the Garden of Eden… I felt gratitude for Yun's gentleness. Because of this, I indulge myself and become happier, almost virginal again. I told Yun about my hope for rebirth. However, it seems that Yun does not feel the same way. Why did my hope for a new life trigger something uncomfortable within him? Was it because I did not express my gratitude to him at first, because I expressed my happiness first? I got my punishment straight away, when he ridiculed, "You are delusional. You have had several men, you've already given birth to a boy. How can you feel virginal?" Yun's words upset me, and reduced my worth. Surely he knew I meant metaphorically virginal, full of hope?

That night, we were supposed to feel joy after we made love. We should have enjoyed our night together, relaxed, and sweet with intimate talk. No, it was arguing and bickering.

Yun changed the mood, by asking, "If I had affairs during my time in China, how would you feel?" How can he ask me this; the mother to his baby son, a mother who takes care of his son, while working hard to support our son, a female patient, who just had half her body mutilate by surgery? He seemed to have asked this just to create tension, as he had told me that he does not believe in affairs. His tone was sarcastic and arrogant, as was his body language. He wanted to hurt me. Because of his attitude and the direction of the conversation, the door had been opened, and I had to ask if he had had affairs. When I did, I was desperate with hope that he would reassure me that it was I who he loved. He had been waiting for the question and smugly told me of all the women who he had recently slept with. This was both before and after I was sick. His words, like a sharp sword, pierced me. His indifference was like the sword being withdrawn from my body, and the blood that spurted out of me was his laughter.

Before I knew that I was sick, there was one time when I did ask him if he had slept with other women. He denied having any affairs. Now he admits to having other women, as if it was his way to sabotage the relationship. He did not have the courage to end it himself. He knew that by telling me the truth that I will turn away from him. Now my body is revolting that he wanted out. It was as if it was my fault that my body was sick, and that he wanted take revenge on me.

Because I want to still treat him with respect, I did not ask with aggression, I was calm and open. I put my dignity and pride in that question. Yun, being the man that he is, will not show sympathy to a weak partner, but he will shrink in front of a strong person. He did fall in love with me, and then because of that love, felt trapped and tried to repress his feelings. He hates my pride and dignity, and now because of my sickness, belittles me. I know this, I have seen it before and it makes my heart sick. Being a woman can be difficult, especially when the man detests a woman's strength and pride. I cannot change this – I cannot relinquish my pride and needs as a woman. There must be men out there who are compassionate and understand a woman like me.

Even when I was pregnant, and with the birth of our son, he took every opportunity to reduce my dignity. Should a seriously sick person, especially a seriously sick woman, lose her natural way of being proud and strong?

I did not sleep that night, I shed tears for my son. In the morning, I go to the bathroom and try to improve my appearance. I look at the long scars on my body. Yun pushes open the door, "Let me see your scars."

We, a man and a woman, previously full of passion; with that passion, we created our son. Now my body needs him more than ever, but my heart and his are separated by a barrier.

There is a wall between us. It's like the threshold between our bathroom and the corridor. If you crossed over, you can become clean in the white bathroom, you can wash yourself clean and refresh. Then you may forgive all the dirtiness. However, Yun stepped half in and half out over the threshold. It's like his personality, half genuine, half hypocritical.

I want to close the door to stop him from seeing my grotesque body. I want him to keep his distance. I want him, but I do not. He stands at the doorway. My stark-red scar exposed to his eyes in the morning sunlight. He is about to say something, but stops.

A cute lovely son, with a lively personality, who is growing every day, every year. What does this mean to a woman? It means to me that I will have a lifetime connection with a man – my son.

I love my son, and during my son's growth, some of his father's character emerges. Does not matter if it is good or bad, but reminds me of the connection, all the past love and hate. A lifetime of experience and tragedy, on this long life journey, does make one wiser, and perhaps more understanding.

Even after what he told me, my sleepless and sick body does not want leave him. I want him to come with us to buy clothes for Tantan. I want to go with him to buy presents for the children of the art group. Although, hand in hand, we fought the entire night. Yun, with his arm gently around my waist; it felt sweet, comfortable. On that day, I follow Yun – as if he is my only hope, even though he told me that he slept with other women whilst I was sick. I still want to remain with him. Where is my dignity?

When we passed by an ATM, I withdraw 500 German marks (the currency on that time). Even when withdrawing the money I still have Yun's words in my head. I returned to Yun and we continued walking, where I snuggled into him. A moment later, I realised that I had forgotten to take the money. I hurried back to the ATM. The money was gone, taken by some lucky person.

In the cold wind, my healing body is in pain – I forgot the money. Since this cancer, and three surgeries, plus chemotherapy, and radiotherapy, the pain of my body slowly recedes with time. However, the pain I felt when Yun told me that he slept with other women remained deep within my soul. This is worse than the cancer pain, the surgery pain. But I cannot give him up. There is still love in my heart for him. I am struggling.

Spring, summer, autumn and then winter; I am recovering. The routine checkups show that all results are normal. For the year of 2001 my relationship with Yun is like a cloud in the sky, sometimes close, sometimes far away. I gave up my marriage with Jim for this man, to father our son; I hoped inside that Yun would treat me well, if so, it would have been worth giving up my marriage. But destiny played its ugly hand. There are always emotional barriers and I cannot forget his being with other women. Since the cancer, Yun was reluctant but he finally commuted between Berlin and Beijing. Every time he felt guilty about his behaviour, he showed me more love. I was touched by this.

Tantan is our bridge; the life we created in one night has tied us together. In December, Yun returned to Berlin to spend Christmas with us. During that time Tantan sometimes hung on to me, sometimes on to Yun, and he laughed like an open-mouthed Buddha – we three were a family and difficult to divide. I have a family. There is our two-year-old son, and the warmth of Yun.

Two years after surgery is a vulnerable time, I cannot relax. At the beginning of 2002, I start running in a forest park. I want to support my healing.

For the cancer treatment, I had three surgeries, then chemotherapy and radiotherapy. Although I loved my career, I would have liked to put it on hold until I recovered. But I couldn't, as Tantan and I needed the money to live, so I kept working. It did not matter that my face was blue and dark green from the medication I was being pumped with, or that because of the disease or the drugs I was myopic. It was my friends who told me. One said that it was like a poisonous gas that I was being treated with. At the time he said nothing as he did not want to make me sad. It took several years before my face returned to its normal colour.

My mother saw this as well, and it was around the time when her hair turned white with worry for me. Her back also had stiffened with tension.

The Chinese Spring Festival is a time of family gatherings. At sixteen years of age I was at university, and did not live with my parents, but returned during the summer and winter holiday periods. After I went to Germany, I did not celebrate one Spring Festival with my parents. In my youth, I cared little for the occasion, but now, in my late-thirties, tradition called. I yearned for my family and those times. Because of this, my parents came to Germany to look after me for a time.

After Christmas, Yun went back to Beijing. On New Year's Eve he called me. I was happy as he told Tantan stories nonstop. He then asked me to guess who his special guest was. Being family time, apart from my mother, who else could be there? I was confused. Then suddenly my younger sister's laughter rang out.

After she took the phone, she told me that she was passing through Beijing, on the way to North-East China to go skiing with her colleagues. She decided to spend the New Year with Yun. Hearing this I felt warm, and the love of family passed through my body. I love my sister and family love is connected through blood, and I was pleased.

Later though, my wise mother was upset and said, "Your sister is a fool! How could she go to Yun's place to spend the New Year with him... it's inappropriate". I laughed at my mother, thinking she is being old fashioned. My sister and I have the same parents, she also has her own husband, and a son only a few years older than Tantan. My sister would not do anything to hurt me, and would support Yun in a sisterly way, and watch Yun to ensure he did not take up with other women.

A few days later, I put a call through to my younger sister. I told her of Mother's traditional thoughts. With a laugh, I asked her if she witnessed any dishonest behaviour from Yun. "No", she said confidently, "I think he is being faithful". I had always trusted her and saw no reason not to do so then. We giggled, like sisters do. She said she has a secret assignment… to watch him for me.

Up until that time, I had received a phone call from Yun every two or three days. After that though, I did not receive one from him for about a month. I wanted to call him, but I felt that if there was a problem my sister would report on him. I was anxious as I should not have to ask another woman to watch over my man, and this included my younger sister. Why do people allow themselves to say things that do not feel right in their heart, to do what they do not want for themselves? They indulge themselves. Was this because I was sick? Since the cancer, until now, I seemed to be more scared. I was weak and did not admit it to myself. Thinking about it, I made my mind up not to ask or question any more – I will concentrate on the treatment of this disease, and take care of my son.

A month after the Chinese Spring Festival, Yun returned to Berlin. His news was shocking; my young sister had fallen in love with him. I collapsed on the couch. As he stood there, he told me that at first it was not he who wanted my sister. It was her fault. But now he wants to marry her.

I was devastated. I divorced for Yun. I had his son; I wanted to marry him. Now he whacks me with the news, "I want to marry your sister". I, in a controlled voice as possible argue, "Yun, we must be together, we have a son to bring up… My sister is married and has a son. You need to consider this very carefully. I will try and be patient and wait for your answer".

Yun stood still, he touched me gently and said, "That was only a moments' love, it's already finished. It means nothing". Yun had never married. I knew he often said to a woman he had just been with that he would marry her.

What does it mean when a man describes a relationship with a woman and he uses the word 'pure'? To my understanding that means Yun has no sexual relationship with my younger sister. This was from his mouth.

I'm unable to bring myself to ask, *Yun, be honest, did you sleep with my sister?*

These words should come out any women's mouth, if faced with this proposition. But I keep silent. My heart aches. Pain, there is no place for me in Haven – pain, there is no place for me in Hell, and the night of darkness is long, I don't know if I still have the ability to love in the future.

My mother now hates Yun. She thinks that her two daughters both died by his hands. He has damaged me, and sullied my sister. She thinks Yun never really loved me – nor my sister. He has always been jealous of me, unable to bear me. This was his way to break me by using my younger sister. My mother saw her two daughters fall by a devil-man's hands. She turned white overnight, such was her grief. This was to happen only in the future.

That night, no one slept. In the morning, I put on my tracksuit and shoes and headed out for a jog in the forest. Tears blurred the path.

No, I don't know how I learnt to be rational. This is hypocritical. I was trained to not express emotion, to accept cultural norms. I learnt though; being one's self, respectfully, is to gain people's admiration.

I am angry, I am in pain, crushed. This news was thousands of times scarier than the cancer declaration – ten thousand times more evil than cancer. We are sisters from the same womb, the same parents. Not only that, we were friends, we never fought. Being my only younger sister, I was always supportive of her. She has fallen in love with Yun in the short time when Yun did not contact me. I trusted her, entrusted her to watch Yun.

Still, I cannot hate him. No matter how much he fought with me or bruised me emotionally. Together, in love, we created our son Tantan – this hooks deeply within me. It was only two months ago that Yun and I walked hands in hands. Now, two months later, he has fallen in love with my younger sister.

As we lie in my bed, the bed that we had made love in hundreds of times, where he had told me he loves me, it is here, lying together, where he gives me this news. He is confused, and feeling guilty. I can't endure this anymore and descend into a cave of darkness.

Yun assures me that he will break up with my sister. I am not sure how I feel about this. I should phone my sister; after all, I am the eldest, but my pride is too wall-like. However, my mother called her. She then told me that my sister said she did not have an affair with Yun. I did not know if I should believe my mother. Perhaps she is trying to settle my mind that my sister was not the one who seduced Yun. Yun is a male, you cannot easily trust a male, your sister had no desire to have an affair with him.

I trusted my sister.

This was the time when Yun had no contact with me, not even for our Labour Festival. Nor did he answer his phone when I called him. One time when I called, it was answered. In the background I heard my younger sister's laughter come through the phone… what were they doing there together… "aha, aha, hahaha… aha, aha, hahaha…" Since childhood I am so familiar with that laugh and voice.

During our childhood, we two sisters had such fun, swimming in the Xiang River, or playing and laughing together. After school, we often went fishing, where we learnt that the smellier the creek, the more worms were needed as bait. We would cover our laughing mouths to try to stop the smell. There was one day, when at home we both had sticks and chased each other. In doing so, we smashed a light bulb in the house. Our mother was angry – at first, we were scared and stood statute-still. Until one of us burst out laughing, and the other could not help but also laugh, as we looked at the broken light bulb cord, which was still swinging. The entire village heard our laughter. People often said our voices and laughter were the same. The voice that I am so familiar with was the voice that came out of the phone. I was shocked. The phone connection quickly closed. When I called again, no one answered. I made many calls to Yun's mobile – no answer. Finally, I called my sister's home, and her husband said she had gone to the Huang Mountains.

"Aha, aha, haha… aha, aha, hahaha…" Did my sister's laughing voice come all the way from the mountains? Did it? And into Yun's mobile? Over a thousand miles it must have travelled to his phone, to assault my ears.

This mother, whilst holding her son, was trying to find her son's father. I was crushed. Mother insisted that it was not my sister's laughing voice... that my younger sister would never do such a thing, especially when I was so sick. She said I had become so tense, that I should go to see a psychologist. "My child, you are sick, perhaps with a mental illness... you should better see a doctor". She said this while holding me. She said it several times. I was so confused. I asked myself, am I mental as well as having cancer?

"Aha, aha, haha... aha, aha, hahaha..." The laughing voice kept ringing in my ears. I was unable to sleep. I had a feeling of being burnt and buried alive. After three sleepless nights, I screamed at my parents, "Why...she's my sister... your daughter... he is the father of my son... the shame is on them. Do they not know how they wound me? I do not deserve this sadness. I can't sleep, all I do is to stare at the ceiling". My poor parents just looked at me with sadness. Even so, how could they really understand how I felt? So, I shouted even louder, "Shameless, shameless, shameless", but my parents did not deserve my sadness. I shouted, "Tonight, I am going to find someone to sleep with."

My father, with his grave voice said, "You feel sad, this is for sure. But you have a son. You are a mother. Be a responsible mother... how can you say you want to find someone to sleep with?" His words did not help or comfort me, as to me it just confirmed that they did not understand me, they did not understand my constant pain. This made me even angrier. Again, I shouted, "Yes, I am a mother, so what? If Yun went to a prostitute I would look down on him, he has no right to hurt me. If he had affairs with other women, I would feel betrayed but perhaps I could endure that ... But to have an affair with my sister... that... that is unforgivable. Perhaps if I had a bad relationship with her, or if I did not trust her, if I hated her, then perhaps it would not be as bad... My God, I trusted her so much, yet you do not understand... and, if I trusted her and she has done this, how can I trust anyone from now on? ... And Yun has a son to think of? For him, I divorced my German husband... I have no relatives in Germany. Does my sister consider my son? What about her own son? Her husband? ... What about me? Has she ever considered me, on my virtual deathbed?"

Several times I shouted, all in vain. I hurt so much, I had no control. It is the only way that I can express myself. I cried, my mother cried.

My father tried again when he whimpered, "Don't you commit a sin. Yun does not deserve to be a parent. Don't you sin and make it worse. My grandson is the one who will suffer the most... my little Tantan. Mei, I think you have become mentally deranged. Please go to see a doctor tomorrow".

Again, I wondered if I could have a mental illness.

In a rage, I grabbed my coat and was about to rush out of the door. But then I remembered that I had not slept for three nights, and the blue-green colour of my face, so I went to the mirror to apply some rough. Doing this I noticed a deep and dark shadow in the corner of my left eye. I put more make up on that spot. I was unable to foresee that the dark shadow would remain and never disappear.

DOCTOR TONY

Lenin Square, Berlin.

In my childhood I saw a movie, *Lenin in 1918*. In this part documentary, part propaganda film, spies were plotting to kill Lenin. Bang! Bang!! The sound of guns – then a blank screen. I assumed that the spies had killed Lenin, I was terrified. Then the screen revealed what had happened, ha ha, the spies panicked and ran away. Apparently, at that moment, the screen was to show *Swan Lake*. In China, in those days, censorship forbade the showing of girls in short dresses, so to overcome this, the movie operator placed his hand over the lens until that scene was over. As he did, the entire theatre became dark.

Later, when I became a student at Beijing University, I watched *Swan Lake* at the North-Show-Hall in the Moscow Restaurant. This was performed by the Chinese Central Ballet Group. I kept wondering about what the *Swan Lake* looked like in the movie of *Lenin in 1918;* I wanted to see that movie again. It is a funny thing that when people are denied the chance to see something, they want to see it even more.

After I arrived in Germany, the wall separating East and West Germany was momentously demolished. Some of the socialist names for East Germany were changed back to their original names, some remained, but Lenin Square kept its name. I always enjoyed this square.

It was to this cocktail lounge at the theatre in Lenin Square that I came to hide in. This theatre has a semi-circle design. The cocktail lounge occupied one third of this half-circle building. A few days ago, I had gone there with a girlfriend. On the ticket there was a notice, After the show – redeem this ticket and get a half-price cocktail'. We happily went to have the half-price cocktail. The door of the cocktail lounge was covered by a heavy cloth curtain in the Bauhaus style, simple and thick. We pushed aside the curtain and pushed the solid door open. Inside the hall, we were wrapped by the warm candle lighting. Most of the seats were wide window-side seats with comfortable cushions. The curved walling and candlelight extended further. It was 9.00 pm, and there were still many guests in the lounge. My friend Wuwu and I chose a central place to sit on purpose. Our tickets showed that the half-price cocktails were valid until 10.00 pm. The patrons were all well presented. The men looked confident and stylish, and behaved with decorum; the women elegant. All were relaxed and chatted quietly, with the occasional soft chuckle. The atmosphere, and people, was congenial.

Wuwu and I wondered who these people were. To which class of society did they belong? What were their occupations? Were they models? But we did not think so. Perhaps they were actors? But many actors struggle, these people were prosperous. We are relaxed and enjoy our conjecture. But I have to admit, if I compare the experience of watching a Contemporary German Drama or listening to light music – to do the former, you are pushed to think more. To listen to music, you don't need to think, just relax.

We appreciated the half-price cocktail, and enjoyed watching the guests; we were excited. The number of guests increased, as did the number of waiters serving them. The male waiters were dressed in black shirts and pants. The waitresses wore white shirts, black pants, and a long black apron, which gave them the appearance of being taller than they were. All were young and very cool. When busy, they were efficient. When not so busy they were relaxed and chatted with the patrons. They smiled and seemed comfortable doing so. The lounge hummed with harmony. Wuwu stopped a waiter and enquired who all these people were. Although he was busy, he took the time to explain, with a smile, that the guests were mostly from the broadcasting industry. They were from TV stations, some were editors, or radio anchors, a few were actors and directors. Among them were some friends who were doctors, business people, brokers, etc. Wuwu and I looked at each other with understanding and smiled – this made sense. Wuwu and I agreed to come again to see the pretty people.

Now, sitting here, unexpectedly, only a few days later, I sit in the same seat. This time by myself. After these three sleepless nights, I needed to get out. I did not care about the dark shadow in the corner of my left eye, or how worn out I must have looked. I am certainly not one of the pretty people.

I ask a waiter for a non-alcoholic fruit cocktail. My anger and pain have settled a bit. I watch the people talking with their unconscious smiles. Without concern, I scrutinise them, but by doing so my pain deepens again. I am so broken amongst these happy people. I wish for a sudden landslide to smother a ton of rubble upon me. Before I go to Hell, first I want to see these elegant, and seemingly endlessly happy people.

Not far away, a man walked over to a table, and shook hands with a man there. Staring, I saw the other man stand up and warmly embrace the newcomer. This newcomer was half a head shorter than his friend. Separating, the two men scanned the lounge, and then looked towards me. They came to my table, and asked, in a polite manner, if they could share the table with me. I nodded, but probably without any facial expression. They ordered cocktails, talked warmly to each other and occasionally patted the arm or shoulder of the other. One man stopped talking and said to me in a friendly voice that they were old friends, who met for a drink and catch up.

The taller one was about 185 cm tall, and seemed robust of health. The other was not that short, about 175 cm. It was the shorter one who spoke to me. His friendly tones triggered my curiosity, "May I ask, what your occupations are?" It was the taller of the two who answered, "I'm a salesman of medical instruments", then he pointed to his friend, "He's a doctor". Then he turned to the doctor and said, "Okay, my friend… it's a deal. Now I better go back to my table and guests." They both stood, shook hands, and with a quick hug said goodbye.

The doctor sat down and asked a waiter for another drink. Once in his hand, he raised his glass towards me, "Prost… I'm driving and can only have one drink. Look, my friend has lot of friends, I came here by myself… it looks like you are by yourself as well?"

I smiled in acknowledgement.

"Before, I wondered if once I finish talking to my friend, would I like to sit with you for a while… that's why we came to your table". He looked at my glass and asked, "What about you? Are you driving and aren't drinking alcohol?" His tone was relaxed and friendly.

"I don't drive. I would like alcohol but my body won't allow it at the moment".

"Why, may I ask?" His eyes filled with professional care.

"I have problems with my intestines. Recently I underwent two surgeries. Since then I can't take alcohol. I had cocktails a few days ago here, when I went back home I felt nauseous". There seemed no reason to hide anything.

"Being a doctor, it would seem to me from your face, that you have cancer. Am I right?"

I again nodded, yes.

"But you are so young".

I did not feel uncomfortable. On the contrary, it felt good to be able to talk to someone about it. It was not just the fact that he was a doctor, but I felt I could trust him. *Cancer*, this word coming out of his mouth seemed strange. Better than when it came out of mine. *You are so young...* These words were sour, my unfair fate; tears rolled. Yet, I felt a bit of relief. I restrained myself, forced myself to relax and said, "Sadly, you are right. Thank you for your concern. But let's change the subject". I did not want to discuss my death topic on a night where I am already crying inside.

"Okay, let's get to know each other... I'm Tony, let's not be too formal. What's your name?"

"Mei, my surname is Huang, you can call me either Mei or Huang. Because both my names are short, many German people choose one or the other so I introduce myself like this. So you can choose. In Germany, people are very formal. I am not used to being so formal between friends. In Chinese culture, we do respect our elders with more formal names. Cultures between China and Germany have their own characters. I always feel a bit confused".

"Okay... Mei, Tony is my Christian name. My surname may be too long, and too hard for you to pronounce. Let's just use our simple names, is that okay?" seeing my head nod, he asked, "Where do you come from? Let me guess, you are either Thai, or Chinese. But I think you are Chinese". He looked at me for confirmation.

"You are right, I'm Chinese".

I could see from his eyes that he was pleased with his assumption. "I'm from Poland. I was born in Germany, but my parents went back to Warsaw a few years ago. I have two brothers here in Berlin... I like China. I have read many books about the country. It's good to see that when China opened the door in the 1980s that it developed very well." Tony spoke a lot about China, perhaps showing off his knowledge.

Sipping his drink, he looked at me. He was easy going. I smiled shyly as I never follow politics. He seemed to know more about Chinese history than me. As I did not really offer any opinions, he laughed and said, "Shall we change the topic again?" I wanted to contribute, so I said, "I went to Krakow in Poland not long ago, I liked it very much".

"What did you like about it?" he asked with interest.

I slowly sipped my drink. It felt like I wanted to sip out my reply. Even though I felt sick last time, I ordered a mixture of mango, banana and coconut milk. It is a soft, sweet, sour taste, all at the same time. It calms me. I was enjoying myself and continued. "My friend Biqing had a performance with the Symphony Orchestra of Krakow, she asked me to go as well. I took the train. There were a group of German football fans, without their wives. They talked with me and two other Asian women who were on the train. The next night, at the concert, that group of football fans came to support my friend, and watch the concert. After the show, we all went to the oldest cellar of Krakow to have dinner and a drink – it was a wonderful time. The next day we went to the Auschwitz concentration camp in Oswiecim. The visit was oppressive. My German friends wore a heavy expression. The atmosphere was so different from the one on the train, the concert and the cellar.

I could not stay there and so that night I took the train to Warsaw... Actually, it was my second trip to Poland. The first time I went to Danzig and Poznan... Tony, interrupt me, you know it all. I talk as much about Poland as you did about China!"

"I do not mind you wanting to talk about China".

Tony had another sip. "Okay, which year were you born?"

"1964, why?" I didn't hide my age, but thought a man does not usually ask a lady her age.

"Do you know what big issues happened in China in the year you were born?"

I shrugged.

"In 1964, China exploded its first nuclear bomb. The Chinese government released a statement that China was to develop nuclear weapons for its defence, to break the monopoly of other nuclear countries. It went on to say that they did not intend to use its nuclear power unless an enemy used nuclear weapons first. China is strong." Tony raised his thumb to show it is good, and added, "You must be strong too, as you were born in that year".

"The nuclear explosion, when I was born. Am I honoured as well?" I laughed again, and continued. "There were two other things that happened in the year of my birth. The first is that China had a massive performance called *The Red of Eastern Horizon* in a large theatre with 6000 seats. There was singing, dancing, and poetry recitals".

Tony broke into the song, *The Red of Eastern Horizon*, *"Sun rise up, China has a Mao-Ze Dong"*. After these few lyrics, he looked at me with a cheeky smile "I only know a few words of this song, so only can sing so much".

"You sing the song well, with no accent at all... Years ago, I noticed an interesting fact. China had few songs in that period, and so the people had limited songs to sing or hum.

Often, when Chinese and German friends get together, the Chinese do sing those few songs, and often the Germans know every one of them, and so they enjoy the time together".

"Mei, I like talking with you. You said you have been to Danzig and Poznan. Please tell me how you found these places. I'm keen to hear your thoughts about Poland."

It seems he was not disturbed by my talking of Auschwitz. He is like a friend who has known me for a long time. He looked at me warmly.

I laughed and said, "I first went to Poland in 1994. I went by myself. In Danzig, I tried to find some amber. I even went to beaches to look for the stuff. It was a waste of time. In the end, I brought some cheap amber jewellery. But one night I went and watched Verdi's drama *Nabucco*... The theatre was a simple affair. I will never forget that night or the *Prisoner Chorus*. I was so touched... it was beautiful. I felt that simple theatre matched the drama very well. The king of Cuban Babylon, like the German Nazis, where the cruel intruders who took over Jerusalem and drove the Jews out. In reality, the Nazis took over Poland, so both Jews and Poles were victims. The Poles were not willing to be slaves. When serving their hometown and fighting for their motherland, they sang the *Song of the Prisoners*... their grief and the feeling they bought to the drama still brings tears to my eyes. In my tears, I saw the then German Chanceller, Willy Brandt, go to the Jewish monument for the victims of Warsaw. He knelt down on his knees. He hung his head, knowing that the Nazis in World War II killed them.

The Jews have deeply mourned the holocaust, where they seek atonement by those Nazis. Brandt prayed, "God forgive us, let the souls of suffering be at peace". Brandt, later in 1971 to be awarded the Nobel Peace Prize".

I had been unaware of my tears until one splashed into my glass. I picked up the glass and took a drink. With my tears of the *Song of the Prisoners*, I sang to Tony, *Come, fly, my thought, open your golden wings*, which is also sung in the play.

Tony, holding his glass without sipping, his eyes shining, "Oh Mei, you Chinese, and we Poles are real friends".

Hearing his comment brought even more tears. "Tony, you may laugh at this, but in 1994 I was only ten years old. But I knew a bit of Polish history. Now, I happily wear that amber jewellery from Poland. However, it all changed there a bit later".

"How so?" Tony had the question in his eyes.

"Later, I read the *Danzig trilogy of Grasse*. The history of Danzig was so sad. Poland had not only one Auschwitz-like concentration camp, there was another camp near Danzig. It was because of these camps that I did not stay there overnight. Can that sad time in Poland be expunged from my mind by my escaping back to Germany? No. Sometimes I escape back to China as well. I hid the amber jewellery at the back of my bottom drawer of my cabinet as they may be, not only leaves, petals, spiders, beetles in the amber, there might also be the bones of dead people from the concentration camps.

But I do miss Poland. I must rally myself and go again".

Tony nodded his head in thought. Saying nothing at first, "I would welcome you to Poland. There is more to Poland than that history. My parents' would welcome you as a guest.

You know, I am happy tonight. As a doctor let me tell you of my practice. I run a physio practice where I help patients recover by massage and other treatments. My practice is expanding. I am here tonight to negotiate the purchase of medical equipment with my supplier.

I am touched by chatting with you tonight. You are smart and kind. But I can see from your face, and your black eye socket, that you are far from recovery".

Tony's concern touched me. I did not answer his observation. He looked at me with kindness and sympathy before he said, "Perhaps the pain of illness is just our fate… You still look young. To my observation, maybe the cancer is now controlled and it is possible you will be fully cured.

I want to do something for you. Come with me to my practice, I want to massage you. It really helps, it removes the toxins, and you will relax a bit".

I cannot answer.

He continues, "Do you not trust me? Although my practice is not at the luxury end of the market, and needs work, it will become better in the future. Please… I really want to help you. Normally it is my staff who do the massages… at a cost of 40 Euro an hour. Today, I will do the massage for you, and at no charge. I give you my word that I have no sinister purpose, I only want to help you."

I still cannot find my voice. A few hours ago, I rushed from home to this lounge to escape or forget Yun, forget my sister, to sleep with a man. Now, this time spent with Tony, where my thoughts went to Warsaw, Danzig and Poznan of Poland… my thoughts returned to China, and to 1964, to my birth year… the pain in my heart amazingly has disappeared, my soul returned, all in this short time. But now, when Tony mentioned my illness again, I am not so sure of him. One minute he made me feel good about myself, the next I have concern. But there he sits, opposite of me, with his easy-going way, full of sincerity.

I laughed a bitter laugh. Normally I am not bitter. Even with my health issues, I expect health to return as well as happiness. The bitterness I feel comes from not knowing how to deal with myself with all these issues with Yun and my sister. Most of my life I have tried to live in a positive way to overcome obstacles. However, with the treatment from Yun and my sister, my positivity has collapsed. I have lost trust in the people who are closest to me. Normally, I am positive in everyday things, like study. I work positively, play positively, indulge in sports positively, dancing, skiing, attend concerts positively. But when I think of the ultimate question of life, I am negative. I seldom think of these questions; I have kept these questions hidden. I did not know I was negative on this. When I was in China, most of the time I smiled. When I arrived in Germany, in this more relaxed society, I laughed more often, sometimes I even could not stop laughing. The year I had Tantan, I had a lot more unrestrained laughter. But now this bitter laugh, normally unknown to me, is strange. Again, I smiled bitterly. My conscious mind returned to the reality of this lounge and Tony's question, from its remote travelling. My eyes rest in Tony's hand, which still holds his glass. I am exhausted, both in soul and body. I told my parents that I will sleep with a man tonight, but this was just a desperate plea, to be heard, for a release. I am still staring at his hands.

It became a direct desire, for release. I am hesitant because there are too many bitter things filling my life. These bitter things come from a woman who is terminally ill, bitter from scars on her body and mind. Yet, in my mind, I could be recovering. His hands that are holding the glass, if they massaged my broken body, reaching into my broken soul, to ease away the cancer, heal the wounds from my surgery. Would his hands stop my fear? Would they offer the miracles that I so desperately desire? These thoughts weave through my mind like a snake through a tree. I am unable to speak, and sit in numbness.

I'm like a candle flickering in the night, the thoughts keep coming; I do not want to walk into another white clinic, one that is similar to the stark surgery where so much pain and fear was cut out of and into me. White bed sheets. I do not want to lie down on a cold massage bed...... The resistance came from deep within. Staring at Tony, finally the words come out, "Tony, are you married… do you have a girlfriend?".

He looks surprised by my question. "I am not married, nor do I have a girlfriend at this moment. However, two of my younger brothers were married when they were young. But what does this have to do with my willingness to do a massage… to help you?"

This time my laugh was without bitterness. I felt relief. How strange of me. I hoped he had no wife or girlfriend. How silly of me, I have only just met him. I felt guilty for my question. China has too many flirts. I, having been in Germany for over ten years, knew that German men are also big flirts. Strange, men and females in a pub, drinking and chatting, often ask that harmless question. It is normal. But when I asked this normal question, there was an implication. I still had not answered Tony's question. Perhaps I am too direct, but I cannot help that.

I reply, "I'm divorced, but I have a two-year-old son". Then without thinking I continue, "Do you want to spend the night with me… I mean, we go to a hotel room".

Tony's eyes open in shock. He straightens up his body, before stammering "But, I won't charge you money if we go to my practice and I massage you. If …. If we… we go to a hotel, it's so late… I know where we can book a room, but… I don't have much money in my wallet."

Pushing, I said, "You do not need to worry about money, I have enough. We can go to the hotel by Lake Tegern, they must have rooms… I so desperately need to be held tonight". This last sentence came out more as a whisper. I wanted to forget everything, to hold and be held. I wanted to wake up in Tony's arms, to a blue sky and the blue waters in the Tegern Lake, the white swans. I needed this.

The seconds tick away as he considers. "Mei, listen to me, I can draw money from the ATM. But is your son not waiting for his mama to return, how would you…?" I said nothing. Got up and walked towards the exit.

Tony hurriedly paid his bill and rushed out after me. Catching up, he steered me towards his car. Silently he opened the door for me. I hesitated, standing by the open car door. The wind was cold for a spring night, but it cleared my clogged mind. Tantan's face appeared before my eyes, as well as my father's stern look as I walked out the door – my direction firm.

Tony stood tall beside me said, "You must have some unspeakable worries. I won't ask you more, other than, what do you want to do? Come to my practice for a massage or to the Hotel of Lake Tegern… I will accompany you either way".

I faced Tony and looked into his eyes. They were pure, full of sympathy but overwhelmed. Two strangers who built up trust after a few hours chatting. Tony trusts me and wants to help. This is the basic nature of human beings.

Sometimes this initial kind nature can be manipulated by emotion, desire and self-interest. The cold wind of the spring night swept the street. I gained power from Tony's sympathy, I admired him. I think he admires me. I shake my head, "No… thank you Tony, I think it's best that I go home".

"Good on you. Can I drive you home?"

"No, I will go home by myself, but thank you".

It was not long when a taxi came past. I waved it down. Tony walked with me to the taxi and opened the door for me. He handed over his business card, "Mei, this is my practice, you can come anytime. I will massage you with never a charge".

"Thank you".

The taxi moved on.

IRREVOCABLE BREAK-UP

More dark days assaulted me.

One of my friends, tying to comfort me, suggested a movie. We ended up watching a movie that was popular on that stage, *Hilary and Jackie*. I watched without any real interest. The movie recounted the true story of Jacqueline Doppler and her sister, a famous British cellist. Jacky is short for Jacqueline. In the movie, Jacky said to her sister Hilary that she wanted to make love with Hilary's husband. When Hilary warned her to stop these thoughts, Jacky got upset and ran off to an isolated field. Hilary ran after her. Being winter the field was empty. As Jacky ran, she loosened her clothing and in the wind, one item after another floated from her body. Hilary, in panic called after her. She followed the trail of clothes into a forest. She found Jacky, naked and sitting hunched over under a shrub, arms around her knees, her head on her arms crying. Thorns had bloodied her legs. Hilary thought that she was like a small animal that did not know how to protect itself. Lust and loneliness had corrupted her.

Crying, Jacky moaned, "You don't love me, I just want to make love with your husband and you won't allow me to". The heartbroken Hilary took off her coat, wrapped it around her sister, and held her. Hilary said to Jacky that she would allow her to make love with her husband.

This movie emphasised the utmost complexity of humanity, our weakness, jealousy, selfishness, tolerance, deep love, our helplessness, all chaotically mixed up. All over Berlin, the movie was hotly debated. This was also because of the male actor, the hansom, gifted piano player, and music conductor, Daniel Barenboim.

In the autumn of 2000, Barenboim became the Chief Director of Art for *Berlin National Theatre*. Jacqueline is his first wife. Their marriage was lauded as the perfect match. They were both good looking, and artistically talented. The reality was that the marriage was in trouble. When Barenboim left Jacqueline, she was already sick, and died in 1987. The movie must have triggered the memory of Barenboim, where he felt the pain of regret and shame. It was said that at one stage he looked towards the sky and shouted, "God, why didn't I wait until I died to play this movie".

People discussed the story and concluded that it seemed that everything is possible. All standards, morality, and concepts, are without boundaries. The movie may have stimulated the populous to express their thoughts on liberation and control, but the reality is much crueller than the movie. In the movie, the heartbroken younger sister used the compassion of the elder sister to get her way. In my reality, because of the good looks of Yun, I left my German husband. Fate decreed a son to us. Fate expressed the cancer; after the surgery, my body was deformed. Yun is the only person to know my body. He does not like it. My sister has been laying with him, something I could never believe would happen. It was Yun who was supposed to be my emotional support, to my dignity, self-respect, and sex. Life is so weak. Suddenly, like a branch in the cold wind, packed with snow, it can break anytime. Nor do I know if there will be a spring, if there will be new sprouts, greenery, and a time of happiness.

My mother kept saying, "Mei, you need to endure, you need to live. Yun didn't really love your sister; he just used her to upset you, to put you in the grave faster". I do not want to accept my mother's words. Still though, I cannot help thinking that she may be correct. The fate of her two daughter's tears at her heart – in both she saw the weakest and deepest depravity of human nature.

I recognised the iron net that trapped me. I saw that Yun had the capacity to hurt me when he is with other women. And he knew that being with my younger sister was the worst hurt of all. At that time my mother was anxious, because her two daughters were being destroyed by the same man. It was then that her hair turned white – it only took a few days. Normally, she was known to be a strong willed woman. Some years ago she had an operation where they removed her spleen. During the operation she came through because not enough anesthetic had been administered. She did not moan or cry, because her daughters were outside. Now, it is because of her two daughters that she pounded the bed, to express her feelings. After a time her face and fists were red with anger.

Then, my father felt pain in his liver. As I was taking him to a hospital in Berlin for a CT scan, he said, "If it's cancer, don't bother to cure me, I would rather die".

Throughout that spring, the entire family lived under the scare of two lots of cancer and betrayal. We were a broken family, our spirit collapsed. Impulsively, I made the decision that we four should go back to China.

It is all too hard, and although Yun and I fight a lot, and even with the hurt he has heaped upon me, I must see him. I want my son to have a father, all under the same roof again. Whenever Yun and I are together, we are like a pair of hot lovers, but when we are not making love, we fight, all the time – when apart, my heart aches for him.

I said to Yun, "If you love my sister, try it for two years, or even just one year until I recover. Let us give time to prove one way or another if you love my sister". He said he won't wait… there is no need to wait. Pain upon pain, humiliation upon humiliation. Either way, if he said he would wait for my sister, I would feel terrible. If he said he does not want to wait for my sister, that is just as bad. I want him to say he wants me, and not my sister.

Three days later Yun made a phone call to my sister. He insisted that I stand beside him to listen. He clearly said to her, "This relationship is finished". Did I really win back my man? Was this meant to make me happy? Of course not. There were no winners. I heard my sister's crying through the phone.

Actually, my sister and I are both very sensitive people. At that stage, it was hard for us to understand that if the family dynamics were destroyed, then it would be hard to regenerate it.

My sister may have cried but I do not know if she cried out of a lost love or just frustration of not having her way. If it was a lost love, it is likely that she still saw hope in the situation of winning in the end. Also, I wondered how long or hard she would fight for Yun if he were to be her man.

It could not have been easy for her to love Yun, because she had to leave her husband. Did she feel guilt over this? There were good years of love with her husband, but once she fell in love with Yun her feelings for her husband faded.

And what about her child? Sadly, the same applied to her son. In the past, her motherly love and support were as they should be, but lately the child was neglected in both. She ignored the pleas from our parent's, and seemed to ignore the pressure of guilt towards me, her sister. Surely, this must have been eating her.

In order to justify all the hurt she had dished out, she said to Yun that Mei will soon be dead from the cancer. Together, she and Yun will take care of Tantan, along with her child – they will be happy. Such is the mindset and emotions of a man and a woman when in love or when they think they are in love. Especially for a woman, she will put everything into trying to secure the man's love.

But what about the men. Women should know that men are different. At least Yun is not like this. He had feelings for my sister. He told me this to pin more pain on me. He said with hate in his voice that my sister's love for him is better than mine. But Yun, when he is with me, unconsciously shows me love. After he does, he feels annoyed with himself. Perhaps my sister is his best bet, as she worships him. She takes in every word he says, and panders to his needs. Yun, with his ego, enjoys the adulation, and her obedience. He did not seem know that to support his woman, he needed to be gentler emotionally, and absorb some pressure. He did not comprehend that obedience and gentleness of a woman is not the way to win a man's heart.

He expects that it's so easy for him to leave my sister. He expects to have a family and decorate the home nicely. Yun, Tantan, and I live again as a family. Things settle, we laugh again. Yun plays with Tantan. His best game is where the boy rides on Yun shoulders. Yun, though, does not seem to know that once the heart is ripped out, the wound is hard to heal and needs time. I have doubts about Yun and my sister, the worry lingers. On the surface things seem fine but I deplore his behaviour.

Yun did not seem to understand his careless behaviour. He thought that it was just a matter of breaking it off with my sister, returning to me; all would be forgotten and I should show gratitude to him for his return. However, I could not endure this dirty relationship. I struggled all the time. Even though I was sick, I insisted on leaving Yun. Yun knew my weakness. If I didn't take him back, he would go to love my sister. This would be enough to hurt me. I continuously imagined what happened and what could happen. My mind did not stop. This was no way to recover from cancer.

The marble statue of *Laocoön* and his sons in the Art Museum in The Vatican keeps appearing before my eyes. Agsandros, with the help of other artist, created the statue around the first century BC. Laocoön was in the middle, appeared to be in either extreme fear or pain, perhaps both. He was trying to save himself and his two sons from two massive snakes. In his left hand, he grabbed one of the serpents, but its sabre-like teeth still bit into his hip. His elder son, on his left, seems not to be wounded, but is terrified, and tries to disengage the one snake where its lower length had encircled his foot several times. His younger son on his right was bound by the other snake and was helpless. Laocoön raised his right arm in despair. The anguish on the faces of the three, coupled with the tensing of the muscles, reflected grotesque spasm. The statue expresses the extreme tension of people when under great duress.

In Greek Mythology, 13th Century BCE, during The Trojan War the Greeks held the city of Troy (in modern day Turkey) under siege for ten years. Their last gambit was to make it like they had given up and left the battlefield, presumably to return to Greece. At the site, they left a house-sized wooded horse. Hidden within were Greek solders. The people of Troy, thinking the Greeks had withdrawn, were amazed and flummoxed by the horse. They thought it must have been a gift. Homer's Iliad describes that the wooden horse was dragged onto the city of Troy. At night, the hidden soldiers crept out and unlocked the massive city gates. Once opened, the Greek army, who had come out of the hills, rushed in and sacked the city. It was Laocoön who foresaw the folly of bringing the horse into the city. This upset Athena's and Gods' plan to destroy Troy. It was Athena who sent the two giant snakes to attack Laocoön and his sons to kill them.

When the statue was discovered, the right hand of Laocoön was missing, as was a hand on each of both sons. The statue has been repaired. There are theories on why the hands were missing, but no one knows for sure.

Grappling with my issues, I could have been Laocoön, such was my torment. The statue could have been made of me. My soul and body distorted in pain. The handless sons is like my situation, where I have lost both Yun and my younger sister. Where I was trapped in this fate.

There are so many times the nightmare disturbs my dream. I am swirling, and I see a few girl friends from my youth, all having affairs with Yun. In the dream, they slept with Yun, but ignored me, as if I was not there. My anguish makes them feel that they are stronger than I am; they feel happy because of this. They all have grotesque smiles on their faces, because they see weak people's pain. In the dream I try to reason with Yun, "how could you do this", but my voice is mute. Nothing comes out. My frustration wakes me up.

Once awake, I would recover my emotions and self-control. A few years later, every time when I saw any other sister combination, who were close to each other, I felt uncomfortable. I once had loving feelings with my sister, our parent's daughters. We trusted each other, and we could talk about any subject without rancour. When I heard that she spent the Chinese New Year with Yun, I was pleased, as the New Year is family time. Now, knowing what had happened I regretted that I gave my approval. I could not trust sisterly love any more.

A few years later, I could feel happy, sometimes real joy, but the trust is gone – faith in people is gone – my heart is no longer there.

Yun was blamed. He broke my sister's family. Apparently, he was happy to believe and hear my sister say to him that she had no feelings for her husband. Yun said that she told him this. He may be a bad partner but he seldom lies.

When I first met Yun, he told me that his parents were divorced. So from a young age there was no father in the house. He said that if he ever had a child, he would make sure there was a happy family unit. I was moved by his words. Once I was pregnant, I told Jim that I would divorce Jim. This I was prepared to do for my baby and a cohesive family. Before Tantan was born, I divorced my husband. I then had Tantan, and a year later cancer, surgery, and a deformed body. Then Yun told me that he had slept with other women whilst I was pregnant. And now he falls in love with my sister. My sister then divorced. If that was not enough, Yun told me that he is again sleeping with other women. I was not surprised, but it still stabbed. The heart is to be the judge.

Time passed by, the cancer, surgery, chemotherapy, radiotherapy, a part of my life. I spent the next two years, which are the high-risk years when the cancer can reclaim me working to make money for my family, growing our son, and trying to digest the affairs between Yun and my sister, and Yun's other affairs.

One of Yun's colleagues told me that Yun still kept up the relationship with my sister. And, at Yun's office, I was sure that he was having an affair with his German female colleague. I hoped these were not true.

Most people are like fish in a big tank, where daily they are fed. Some feel secure in the tank. I am also a fish but I was hurt badly. I decided to leave the tank and return to my sea to live independently.

We have our son, and there has been no marriage. Even though I showed Yun my divorce papers, we are still not married. I divorced a man who loved me, and I was happy with him in many respects. My Jim was the only person who I could depend on in Germany.

I get to the point, or I think I do, where I no longer care who has affairs with Yun, including my sister. Sea, could I dive under you again? Mountain, could I run through your snow again? Dance hall, will you feel my moving feet on your floor?

I HATE MY BODY

"What is a man-made anus", I asked before the operation. I had no idea what I would end up with. I was afraid to find out. Then after the op, for the first few days when confined to bed, a nurse had to manhandle my body, to wash me, clean the sheets. As she rolled and manipulated me I was indifferent towards my body, I did not want to think about it. I pretended that I did not care.

When I woke up from the first surgery, the doctor told me that in order to save my young life, to get rid of all the cancer, my anus had been removed. Now I had a man-made anus.

A few days later, after I started to recover, my mind started to recover as well. When the nurse helped me stand, she said, "Ms. Huang, from today you need to learn how to deal with your man-made anus. You must learn how to wipe it and keep it clean". I was reluctant.

Then I saw it. A pink soft fabricated hole. I almost asphyxiated. I looked at the nurse, helpless, afraid, and horrified. I took a deep breath, for air, and to breathe in strength. Okay, I can handle this, I need to accept my fate. I did not scream, I did not cry.

The nurse was business-like, but gentle. She did not give me the chance to be weak, and started to help me clean the man-made hole. I turn my head away because of the smell. For days I cannot get use to this thing, but the nurse is firm, "This is now your body. You need to take responsibility for it. I only can help you whilst you are in here. You will be dealing with it for the rest of your life, so get use to it".

Reluctantly, I start to take responsibility for it. A few days later, I ask the nurse how long is this fabricated anus likely to last? As part of my accepting it, I want to know if it will last me out, and, what it will look like when I am old.

The nurse is gentle with her answer, "I knew a patient like you, and after twenty years she still has her man-made and it was working fine. You had a big operation, and now you are not the same as a normal person. But if you adapt with the right attitude, you will be fine."

I had to accept that I had stage four cancer. The operations saved my life. This now is a consequence. I remember seeing people on TV who had lost their hands, or were born without hands; they used their toes to wave, to eat. Life is a miracle. I am horrified almost every day, how can I keep on going with my life?

I cut off my relationship with Yun, completely. I divorced myself from my body – both are gone. I became a single mother with cancer. Before I laid on the operation table, I loved my body. I opened my mind to my imperfect form. I and my body rely on each other, no matter there being a loss of dignity or in humiliation. I broke up with Yun, which made me cut off my bodily connection with Yun. I felt lost, full of fear and weakness. I can feel there are two locks on my body. One lock is of self-confidence. The birth of Tantan made me strongly want to be connected with his father. The other block is one of my own mind. I hate what my body has become. How can I offer it to a man? These two blocks play heavily on me. I lost Yun and my sister, just like I lost my anus. The measure of being human is of fortitude. Mine is gone, or at least well hidden. If I cannot break through this evil grip, where is my self-value? I would flounder into a bitter sea without a shoreline, drowned in self-pity. It is a function of humanity to fight for life, as the tiger would when he wants to consume you. The struggle is innate, we fight for every breath. Some are stronger than others. I must be the strongest – the choice is mine alone to make. Life is long, keep moving and the soul will emerge, the heart will be cleansed.

Once, when in Southern China, I saw a lake at night. Yet, there were colourful lights that moved around. Boats on the lake carried the lights. Everything was so quiet, not a sound from the boats, and the boats themselves were too dark to be seen, so it seemed that the lights floated on the water.

A lot of times when in a person's life, the light of pursuing perfection is turned off, you would be like a boat moving on the dark sea: if you smash against rocks, you would be destroyed. If you kept your fighting spirit inside, and turn on the light again, your rescue boat will arrive to carry you to the oasis. People normally have several aspects to their character. Some people are good at multi-characters, some people are happy to be multi-characters. Some people have multi-characters unconsciously. Some people feel helpless to have multi-characters. For the woman who experiences the pain of menstruation, love, abortion, marriage, divorce, giving birth, their life would show the changing faces, such as in Sichuan Opera (a Chinese Opera), where she, the actress, would sit with the audience to watch the changing faces of the actors in the opera.

I was sixteen when I aborted my first child. It occurred during my first love. I had to endure the disdain in the eyes of the nurse. After the abortion, I ran like I was flying to my boyfriend. After a few days my body pain was gone. However, the pain of letting go of the little one is forever. Too often a little body appears in my dream, vaguely to touch, and reluctant to leave. A never-healing scar to my soul. Then in Germany, as an overseas student, I married into a prosperous family. But I was not satisfied with the life of a bourgeois wife, doing nothing; I was unfaithful to my character. Then things happened so quickly, too many changes: pregnant, a child, cancer operations, fear, death of mine, a single mother, divorced, loss of my anus – I was lost. I accepted these things, but the weight of purgatory I could not accept.

I hoped that my life would begin again once I broke up with Yun and became a single mother. I wanted to heal my ailing body to choose dignity and freedom. I wanted to break free those blocks and not fall in the trap of weakness. I wanted to win the battle against fear. I wanted to find the light to keep on going.

On the 1st January 2001, I was in front of my computer. The first day of the new year, I needed to restart work.

From the day I walked into hospital for my surgery, until the time I walked out, twelve days passed. When I walked out of the hospital, most of the intravenous lines had been removed. A few others were to be taken out in a few days. In 2000, the start of the new Millennium, I was out of the hospital, and ready to start living again. There were no bells ringing in the hospital, but there were bell ringing all over the world – the sound of the new Millennium.

Jim thought that I would die, but I did not die.

When people escape the gate of death, they know how to live more fully. I did not want to die, I wanted to listen to the last bell sound of 2000. I wanted to start a new life journey, irrespective of my body being mutilated for the rest of my life.

RETURN TO WORK WITH PAIN OF BODY

I had my German passport, but never wanted to use social welfare. Most German's take it for granted. Those people who took social welfare would sit in a chair at the office of social bureau, and blame the government that they cannot find a job… that the government must create more jobs, but better jobs – cleaning, and garbage collecting, are jobs for Poles and Yugoslavs. The social welfare staff have to listen to their complaints, day in and day out, and offer comfort to them.

Barbee was a young, beautiful girl, who completed her university at twenty-eight, and worked for two years. Unfortunately, at thirty, she had a car accident, which left her disabled. As a result, she became neurotic, and her hands constantly shook. She also had difficulty concentrating. Her parents' friend was a headmaster of a music school. He lent Barbee an accordion and encouraged her to play it, of course whilst learning music. He hoped that the practice would help her overcame the shaking of her hands. Perhaps, it would may also improve her concentration. Barbee had medical insurance that paid for her tuition. In time, she started to get the hang of it. After six years of playing the accordion, her hand shaking stopped, and her concentration improved. The music improved her confidence, she found love, and married. Her husband was a handsome bank manager with a good income. Now, twelve years later, Barbee lived a happy life. She took pride in her home, keeping it well furnished and tidy.

In order to have an easy life, she decided not got to work, and applied to be assessed for 100% disability, which she now received. Barbee loved art. Because of her full disability pension, she could go to art museums, to concerts, with discounted tickets. Her husband, as the supportive person, also enjoyed the discounted ticket.

Barbee played the accordion well. She was capable of simple work, but she did not want to work. She wanted the 100% disability pension.

Whenever I met Barbee and her husband in a gallery, or at a concert, I did not know if I admired or despise them. I do not think I feel this way because of the success I have gained. Especially once I escaped the death gate.

For myself, I cannot accept doing prosaic work, which does not call on my creativity. It is not just the ability to earn money. During the chemotherapy period, with having to hold and carry the Chemo bottle, twenty-four hours a day, I still ran around, going to the law firm, and notary office, so I could register my small culture company. Not once did I ask for even one cent from social welfare. On the contrary, I created job opportunities for the German society. Because of the high unemployment rate of Germany at that time, job creation was so important.

When my small company sent a recruitment request to the labour bureau, they often sent more than ten applicants. Sometimes, up to a hundred came. I remembered the time when Jim sent out his resume to apply for a job without luck. I read all these CV's that came to me, more than one time, I read their educational background, employment history, qualifications – all good quality candidates. I found that most of the candidates were over qualified. This posed a problem as the requirement and salary was lower than what most of these people aspired to. I can appreciate the agony of those over-qualified people for having to do work that is below their qualifications and income level.

To start a company, what does providing job opportunities mean? I only had a small culture company, therefore I only had limited experience, but this experience was direct. I required a bookkeeper. This person would also do the taxation requirements. Normally, I would be fine to do this work myself, but I could not get my head around the German documentation – I did not want to make mistakes.

Even with stage four cancer I was active in wanting to produce my own income. Also, the harder I worked, the greater the pressures, the more I would feel Jim's appreciation. Jim never treated me as a homemaker, whose sole purpose is to do all the housework, and service her husband. Jim respected my abilities.

However, a few years later, I cannot stop demeaning myself. Actually, when Jim faced unemployment pressures, I did not give him enough compassion and support. There are two reasons; one is because I had not experienced the scary factor of possibly losing a job. The second reason was that I was too arrogant, I did not have enough tolerance. I believed myself to be capable, and could see that others may not have trusted themselves enough. I was amazed that he could lose his position.

It may be because I had Jim's love in the past, because I loved, and still have this love, I would never give up.

At university, I read a speech named *Motivation for Exploration*, which was written by Albert Einstein. This was read at Max Planck's birthday party. It influenced me very much, and went something like; Einstein said, *'There are many rooms in the science temple, and many people live in them. The motivation guiding each person is different. Many people like science, because science gives them a happy experience for their intelligence. Science is their entertainment. In this entertainment, they look for an active experience, to successfully satisfy their aims. In the science temple, many contribute their products of wisdom to the altar, their purpose is for interest only'.* Einstein said, *'If there is a day that God sends an angel to earth, the angel can expel the above two kinds of people. Although among these two kinds, there are many excellent people'.*

On the first day of January, I sat in front of my computer to work. My wound hurt. I grabbed a soft pillow and held it against my wound. Yet, I was excited. *The People's Art Publishing House of China* was holding a nationwide *Xiangyun Cup* children's painting competition. One hundred paintings were selected from 20,000 pieces to bring to Berlin to exhibit. I was part of the organising committee, and liaised with the Art Department of the University of Berlin – one of the most famous Art Faculties in Europe. They also were to host this exhibition. The representative group was made up of students and teachers, who were to attend the opening ceremony. There was only one month left for me to complete all my functions.

I had to write a piece, covering each of the one hundred works, both in Chinese and German – along with the artist's name, age, gender, etc. I had to do an overview of the Chinese children, and that they came from twenty-five different provinces of China, and from over fifty Chinese nationalities.

These works were young but brave, with emerging skill. I enjoyed the connection to the works and our motherland, reflecting both customs and contemporary views. I forgot my pain and health issues, as I sunk into the work, proud, and with tears of joy.

At the beginning of February, the visiting group of more than thirty members arrived in Berlin. I was there to welcome them. I had taken the time to buy gifts for children at Kaufhaus Des Westens.

At that time Kaufhaus Des Westens was the biggest shopping complex in Europe, with six floors of shops. Everything could be purchased there; cosmetics, jewellery, fashion and clothes, books, CD's, appliances, furniture, everything.

Sitting under a palm tree there, the busy city views were to be had. There was the "Broke Head Classroom" not very far away. In World War II, the allied forces destroyed it. Now it is a Kaffee Haus, offering the beauty and power of its broken past, where many now sit and enjoy their coffee.

There was a corner at Kaufhaus Des Westens. I loved this corner and used it often. A decade later, with Kaufhaus Des Westens refurbished, the corner has sadly gone. On level three, in the book area, there was a small shop that sold old stamps. The stamps were sold in bulk, and by weight. 50g, 100g, 200g, 500g. They came from all over the world, Germany, Eastern Europe, Western Europe, Asian, African, Latin American, etc. There were different interests, such as before World War II, and after World War II. Every stamp had history, a story. Every stamp had a special picture. The best for me was that you could buy an envelope with up to one hundred stamps for only a few marks. It was the stamps that I chose for the children.

In the envelope, it was not easy to determine what the themes or periods were. There was a plastic window in the envelope and I shook the envelope and peered into the window, and shook again, to get more stamps to show themselves. These stamps bought a smile to the faces of the children; I heard their surprise and delight.

In the afternoon, at the education faculty of the Berlin Art Campus, the Chinese Children's exhibition opened. Gifted young musicians performed as part of the opening. Although I made my face up, the colour on my face was still brown. I saw this from photos later.

Tantan, who was only one and half, stood beside me. I would not sit down and stood with the rest of the audience to show respect to the musicians; that was the first time I stood without moving for over an hour after the operation.

On the day when the artistic group left, I started my chemotherapy. There was no pain or skin irritation from the chemotherapy, but I was deeply fatigued. Nevertheless, I still worked on my computer, but had to lie on the bed often to rest. Then I understood why the doctor did not want me to have the chemotherapy immediately after the surgery. After surgery, my heart is full of fear and I am filled with horror of my heart being weakened. In my younger days, I seldom read books relating to health issues. I spend all my time on romantic themes, on love and dreams. I am worried. My body is full of cancer cells. I am afraid that maybe somewhere in my body, a cancer cell or two is hiding, and that these cancer cells are not afraid of the chemo, hiding behind cover, waiting, ready to strike me down again. Everyone has cancer cells in his or her body, but the immune system normally takes care of them. Everyday, our body metabolism works to suppress cancer cells from multiplying. Now, after my surgery, I am weak. I have to accumulate my strength, and recover, before the destroying effect of chemotherapy.

Although I am afraid of the relapse of cancer, I am keen to work, to occupy my mind and keep motivated. A good mood is the best medicine, so I am told. If I do not work, I will have no income.

With my German nationality, I am entitled to welfare. But even when sick, I do not apply for it. I cannot take it for granted, like some Germans; first, I have to contribute to this country, to this society. And although very weak, I want to work so I feel life.

Of course, work is not my entire life. I still love many things. The chemo starts, and in the process *The Fiftieth Berlin Movie Festival* starts. I do not want miss it. The doctor advises that a good mood is the best medicine. I am a fan of the festival. Can I attend okay? I was going to try.

Last season, when Tantan was only six months old, he had eczema, and could not sleep because he itched all over his body. His small hands tried to rub everywhere. It was horrible. I had to put little gloves on his hands. Only when exhausted would he fall asleep. Usually he slept well from 11.00 pm until around 3.00 am. I went to the festival at 11.00 pm, once he had fallen asleep, leaving him on his own. I rushed back, afraid that he was already awake. I also worried that the police would be at my door because it is unlawful to leave a child under ten years of age at home on their own. Thank goodness, he slept during the few hours when his mother was out.

This year's Festival was also a celebration because of the fifty years of the festival. Being so, it was the first time that a German Chancellor cut the opening ribbon. In February 2001, two months after surgery, my face is a funny colour, my eyes are black, and the pain of my wound as I sit in the cinema is excruciating. Some people I did not know well nodded at me in greeting. But others who knew me well sat beside me in silence.

The chemo, and then radiotherapy, were my best weapons against those rogue cancer cells that I was afraid of. It was important to avoid infection as my immune system was low. That is why they did not do it in hospital, with the normal intravenous infusion. Instead, I could have the chemo at home, the doctor performed an operation on my chest to insert an injection pump that was connected to my blood vessels. To the pump was connected a tube. This attached to a bottle of fluid. The bottle was also elevated. Bottles were fed into me for twenty-four hours a day, for a week. Then I had a three-week break.

Then another week of chemo. The doctor told me that this was the most advanced chemotherapy modality. To me, this was helpful, as I did not need to be at the hospital. In my treatment week, I suspended the bottles while doing some work. On the weekend, I even took Tantan and my parents around on various trains, whilst carrying a bottle. I did this, partly to be a family again, but also, as I wanted to exist again.

Work is my strength, and for me to overcome the cancer I devoted myself even more excitedly to life and work. I embraced life at the same time as doing the chemo and radiation therapy. I completed six phases of chemo. During that time, I had many friends come visit me. We chatted and caught up. Talking with them helped me forget the sickness, and for a time I was able to enjoy life.

When my chemo was halfway through, that was when the radiation therapy started. By the end of spring, I completed twelve sessions of radiation. Once both were completed, the doctor advised that most of the cancer had been cut out, and what remained, with the treatment, would be cured – nor would it return – "you can be a healthy person again". I really wanted to be a healthy person.

SOCIAL DANCING IN BERLIN

There is a Social, Coffee, Dancing Hall in Berlin. It is well attended by adults. I went there once with Jim.

It was well organised in the way that it worked to get partners together. It was also interesting; each person at each table had a telephone and a number. All the single males and females would browse the tables. If they saw someone who was to their fancy, they would take note of the number. Then, from their own table, they would ring the table number and speak directly to the fancied person. As many people would be on the phone at the same time, no one could tell who was chatting to who. The two could talk to each other, and no one would know who spoke to whom, and they would have a private conversation.

There were more to these rules; there was a rotating cylinder that marked, either male or female. When it is the female choice, then a female will invite a male to dance, males cannot refuse. If it is male's choice, he may invite a female to dance, however, the female has the right to refuse.

There were beautiful printed cards on each table as well. On the cards there was a sincere piece of advice; for instance, S*hould a male invite a female then it would be nice to go to the shop and order a rose for the lady. By doing so, the woman is likely to accept the invitation.*

When I first entered the coffee hall, I liked the atmosphere. The males wore suites, females were in nice dresses and lightly perfumed. At that stage, I did not have much money, being a student, and I felt a bit embarrassed that I was not well enough presented, and that my perfume was cheap. Even my age seemed against me, because a quick glance revealed that the guests were confident, and mostly middle age, many with well-shaped bodies. But that was five years ago.

HENDRIK

The dancing hall is much the same. Five years ago, I had a husband who loved me. Sadly, though, the cultural differences were too vast. Then with the short engagement with Yun, I became pregnant. We were supposed to have a life together. But he went back to China, and I made a life for Tantan and myself in Germany.

My body is not the same as before. I cannot wear jeans which show off my belly, for all to see and scoff. I can hide my wounded soul, but I cannot hide the body wound. I wear a dance suite, one that I brought from Beijing. There is a special sash line, which covers my body scar but shows the other side of my waist, which is normal.

Walking through the hall, I look straight ahead, not wanting to catch anyone's eyes, not wanting to be noticed. My nerves are playing aloud. Since becoming a mother, I had seldom participated in social activities. And once sick, I never went outside unless necessary. Since Yun and my sister had their affair, I feel awkward with my old friends. My body and soul are deeply entwined. Now, I have to face a place full of strangers.

After I go through the hall, I walk as far back into the hall as I can and sit down.

I am too nervous to think of dancing – my braveness and strength exhausted. I sit quietly at the back and speak to no one. I feel safer that no one notices me. That way, listening to music, whilst watching the people dance, I relax. It is all I want to do for now.

It seems that even the waiters who serve drinks around me do not see me, as none come to enquire if I want an order. An hour later, I have not even had a glass of water. I get up and leave. I gained strength and pleasure enough from the music and dancing. I will return, I tell myself.

A few days later, I went to the dance hall again. I was not as nervous this time. But I did sit at the back again. A man came over to invite me to dance. I accepted. I wanted to feel 'the dance' again, which I hadn't for a long time. The man only knew the one-two, one-two step and was clumsy. I danced with him to be courteous, but soon suggested that we return to our seats. He escorted me back to my seat. Determinedly, he called the waiter and bought me a drink. He gave a 20 Euro tip and told the waiter to supply me drinks whenever I wanted. The man left. I wondered about this behaviour.

Another man came and invited me to dance. My eyes lit up as I had seen this man on the dance floor earlier, and he was an excellent dancer. Whilst dancing, we exchanged names. His was Hendrik.

After a few songs, Hendrik accompanied me back to my seat. He asked, with a hopeful expression on his face, "May I sit here with you for a while?" I wanted to dance with him again and so said yes. Hendrik sat and called the waiter, he ordered a drink for himself. He saw my half empty glass and asked, "How about another one?" "Thanks, but I still have some."

Hendrik's gentle voice asked, "The man who first danced with you, he paid for your drink?"

"He insisted on paying", I said, and I felt embarrassment redden my face.

It seems that my embarrassment was exactly what Hendrik expected, because he laughed. It was a sincere laugh. I also laughed. This relaxed us a bit and he seemed more comfortable. He said, "Don't worry, I can assure you, all the men who would approach you here would want to dance for relaxation's sake… and will buy you a drink…, it is not for sex, and they will not pester you. You are safe. Ha ha… I know the man who danced with you earlier. He is like that because his dance skills are not very good, so he pays for his dance partners. But he won't pay for all the women, as he only pays for the ones who make him feel good whilst dancing. He wants to show his gratitude. Ha ha!"

I don't know if it was because he told me about this man's secret or if it was because of my embarrassment, but it seems that Hendrik was a bit pleased for having done so. In a relaxed manner, Hendrik put his arm on the back of the lounge we were sitting on, and was very close to me. It seemed strange; when I was dancing with him my hand was naturally on his back, as it should be. Now though, when not dancing, I was embarrassed by his closeness. He seemed one hundred percent relaxed. It was me who was awkward. There was no need to be annoyed by his posture, but I was trying to overcome my shyness. Germany males are normally forward, but most of the times they are kind. Asian women tend to be timid in this situation.

Germans, especially the males, like to show off; they like to show you their knowledge by explaining, analysing, helping, etc. If you understand this when dating, this encourages them even more. I tried to relax and asked Hendrik, "I'm curious. As you seem familiar with people in this dance hall, you must come here often?"

"Ha ha… It has been decades", Hendrik laughed loudly "May I smoke? Just one, it's very mild". I nodded my head, encouraging him to keep talking. He lit up, sucked gently and blew out a long smoke ring, "From the age of seventeen I have come here to dance".

When he saw my surprise, he moved even closer and extended his smile, "Yes, for decades, and I always wear a tie. I like it here".

He flicked the ash off the cigarette and continued, "Honoured lady, for courtesy sake it's not polite to ask your age. But I can guess, because your age is written on your face, hands and body… and when dancing with you, your face was close. I also held your hand and body".

Seemed like he was flirting.

He kept smiling, and his voice was all charm, "And also, you are an Asian lady, Asian ladies look younger, so you are probably older than you look".

I looked blankly at Hendrik but said nothing. I was not going to let too much of myself out. Finishing his cigarette, he stood up, put out his hand for mine, "Come, let's dance". I stood up and pretended to be a lady. As we crossed the floor, I nodded to the singer in greeting. We danced in a big circle, then came back to the front. The music changed to a Cha-Cha. We danced face to face and kept dancing for over an hour. I had not exerted myself much since my operations. I felt dizzy every so often. But seeing Hendrik with such joy on his face, I was determined not to stop until the band had a break. When it did, I thanked Hendrik and left the Hall. My legs were weak and staggered a bit. I was so tired I was surprised, and bit frightened.

A few days later I went to dance again. Hendrik was standing beside the bar and chatting with someone. The bar was the male's world. I greeted him and then walked to my previous seat at the back. Two men came to invite me to dance. Neither were experienced dancers, with only a few steps – not very exciting. I went to the bar to ask Hendrik to dance. He quickly finished his drink and led me to the dance floor.

"Mei, it seems that before the other night I have never seen you in this dance hall?"

"I came here once five years ago and only again recently".

"When did you learn to dance?"

"A few decades ago". When I said these words, I teased him after his previous comments of a few decades. Hendrik laughed, "Good, Mei. You have only been here a few times. You look more confident than the other night… you even made a joke".

My reply was a bit more serious, "You said that you started to dance here when you were seventeen. Do you know that in China, some kids start university when they are only eleven or twelve? Do you believe that? They are geniuses. I myself only spent nine years completing primary and high school. It's not like in Germany, where students spend thirteen years to complete their school. I attended Beijing University at sixteen. I started to learn to dance at the same time. So, I started to dance one year earlier than you. It has also been a few decades. You said you can tell my age, but if you can count, you can work it out".

An apologetic smile came upon Hendrik's face. "Oh, Mei, you are such a good dancer". We continued dancing until it seemed that he remembered something, "Ha, China is a mystery to me. But I worked in Japan for a year. When I came back to Germany, I passed through Shanghai and Hong Kong, where I stayed a week. It's a pity that I have never been to Beijing. I should have stayed longer to see more". After saying this, he seemed to consider something else. He took hold of my hand and led us to my seat. Sitting beside me, he ordered drinks, took out a cigarette, "Like last time, just one. Is that okay?"

Hendrik lit up the smoke, blew another forever-hanging smoke ring, whilst a mysterious gleam occupied his eyes. "When I worked in Japan, I read some books about Japan. But I hardly read anything on China. But I did read one book, it was in English, *Wild Swans*... I interrupted with excitement, "The Chinese name of the book is 鸿, and the author is Rong Zhang, she lives in Britain".

"Yes, yes," he replied, "it is this book. Obviously you read it as well". It seemed that Hendrik was delighted to know that I had read the book. On the other hand, my knowing so much about the book deflated him, as he wanted to share his treasures. I regretted having jumped in so quickly. I should have shut up and let him share, as he wanted to. So to bring him back, I asked with enthusiasm, "Which part interested you the most?" The band restarted to play, and he listened for a moment. Then he looked at me with his big blue-grey eyes. Lowering his gaze, he surprised me by lifting up the tablecloth and in a quizzical way looked at my feet, whilst saying, "The beginning of the book, where Ms. Zhang described her grandmother's bound feet that became so small, like the lotus flower. That amazed me".

"Is that true, that during that period all Chinese women bounded their feet to keep them small? Do they all think that feet like these are beautiful? Or do they just want to make their men happy? Haha, I want to see if Mei has small-lotus feet. I want to take Mei to dance and swirl like a beautiful lotus flower".

On the floor, he twirled and danced me quickly, my dress up like a lotus, my feet like the flower's bloom. Whilst my body danced, my mind was thinking something else. Zhang Rong's book was very successful in Germany and in Europe, in fact all over the world. It was recommended to me by my Post Graduate Master, who was the most senior professor of the university. Hendrik is an engineer and both have read this book, showing how wide the appeal. Many Germans want to understand recent Chinese history through this book.

That night, I danced until I was exhausted. But I enjoyed it. When back home, I kissed Tantan several times while he slept. I whispered, "Mum is getting back her strength, Mum becomes alive again. For you, Mum will be healthy and happy".

Since then I went to the dance hall often. It's a place where I exercise and release the pain from my heart. I do not know when it started, but Hendrik doesn't invite other women to dance any more. He only dances with me. Most nights we leave the hall after an hour or so, and stroll the roads between Kant and Hardenberg Street, where we chat about all sorts of things, deep into the night. Sometimes we go to a cigar bar for a drink. The cigars come from Havana. Hendrik will smoke one, sinking himself into the enjoyment of the cigar. I listen to the music and appreciate the decor of art and craft in French or Havana, South Latin styles.

I always glance at the cinema opposite. In the spring of 1998, Yun and I watched the movie *Burn the Old Summer Palace*. That was the first time when Chinese people watched a Chinese movie in a German cinema. Many people attended. When I was with Yun, I had a closer connection to China. Now that I'm separated from him, China seems far away. After I divorced Jim, it seemed that I had no roots in Germany any more. What about Hendrik?, I wonder as he blows out his big worm-like smoke rings. He suddenly asks, "Mei, what are you thinking?... Are you thinking of China? Actually, I have a close tie with Asia. When I worked in Japan I married a Korean lady."

"Oh" comes out of my thoughts. I look at Hendrik. I am shocked and don't know what to say. My incredulous look makes him laugh so much his shoulders shake, "I divorced her over ten years ago. Our son is now seventeen".

"What does your ex-wife do?" I don't know how much I want to know about Hendrik's ex-wife, but I ask the question anyway.

"She's a painter. A graduate from the art faculty of Berlin Art College"

"A lot of Korean females study music or painting in Berlin. Korean women must be really kind and nice. I remembered a Korean drama series on TV called *Yellow Handcuff*, I watched a few episodes when in China and was addicted to it". When I talk about Korean women being nice and kind, I feel a bit awkward. Actually, I think Chinese woman are probably just as nice and kind as Korean women. I do not know why I feel awkward thinking that Korean women are nicer than Chinese women.

Hendrik has a deep smile, "My ex-wife wasn't like that. Her weight grew faster when she was pregnant, her emotions changed quickly, she even bit me." He does not say this with any spite or malice but indicates that he felt helpless. He speaks as if telling an interesting story but one not related to him, "Although my son lives with his mum, he often visits me… we are good friends. But his mother sometimes acts as if she still cannot get over of me. I don't want to be mistreated by her again. I told her that I can't be with her, and that if she takes good care of our son I will pay a bit more than the allowances the court order allocated. But you must keep away from me… Ha ha". He takes the time to inhale and blow another smoke ring, then pulls a grimace and continues, "You know, I have paid the alimony, and a bit more, so she doesn't make any trouble for me…" while he talks about the payment allowance to his ex-wife, I remember he told me he works for the international company, Siemens. One time, when we danced, I told him that I had a Ph.D. Without elaborating, he mumbled that that he had one as well, but then whirled me in a fast circle. I knew Hendrik was a manager of a small department of Siemens.

Even though divorced and paying alimony, his salary still allows him to dance at the dance hall whenever he wants. He seems not to be concerned about paying for our drinks most of the time, and will not allow me to pay. Yet, he is humble about money. Every time when he pays the bill, he always says with a smile "Only one drink, I can afford it".

When he talked about his past marriage, I felt comfortable; not so much that he's a divorced man, the important thing is, that he is a free man.

One night after Hendrik finished a cigarette in the cigar bar, and I finished my glass of wine, we had our arms around each other as we emerged onto Kant Street. We were excited to be with each other. In the cold wind of early spring, I was drunk and let him go. I ran a bit up the street and shouted out, "Hey Hendrik, do you know something interesting about this Kant Street we are in?... Back in the early 30s and 40s of this century, a lot of Chinese students wanted to rent in this street just because the street name was Kant, who was the great German philosopher."

Later, we arrived at the famous Hotel de Ville on Kant Street. It was late at night, with only a few guests. A waitress was waiting to close the door. Hendrik held me tightly; my skirt and long coat were flapping in the wind. I remembered the photo by the famous photographer, Robert Doisneau, of the two lovers kissing in front of the Hotel de Ville. It is an iconic picture of a boy with windblown hair kissing a slim girl on the Paris street. The photo was thought to be a real scene that Delano randomly captured. But later the truth was revealed. The photo was not a spontaneous event. Apparently, Delano saw a pair of lovers deeply kissing outside a Paris café. This gave him an idea. He asked the pair of lovers to go to the hotel and stage the kiss whilst he took the photo. This did not affect the fact that it became internationally famous, as it is synonymous with the romanticism of the French, especially Paris. Simultaneously, we both headed into the Hotel de Ville. The waitress seeing our happiness smiled and let us in. Her smile was like that Paris girl, hot and attractive.

That entire night we were like young lovers. I expected him to ask me to spend the night with him. But in the normal way, at about 2.00 am, he called a taxi for me. As the gentleman he is, he opened the door for me to enter, as he said goodnight. He even did not ask me when we would next meet. Nor did he have my telephone number, or I had his.

As the taxi drove away, my thoughts rushed, "Does he have other women?" I was not sure about our relationship, but I had no others in my heart at the time. I wished Hendrik felt the same. I was disappointed. Once before, I had experienced a one sided-love affair. I had a crush on a German man. We got along really well, but later I found out he had another girl. I had devoted all my affection to him but did not get the same in return. I was hurt by this and did not want my feelings for Hendrik to be the same. I decided not to allow this to happen.

I understood the whole dance hall situation. There are not many good dancers there. Hendrik knew all of them. There were a few good dancers but in pairs. They seldom danced with others. There was a man named Godlier who was an excellent dancer who I wanted to dance with. He came by himself and danced with the better lady dancers. There was one night, Hendrik and I were standing near the entrance, off the dance floor, when Godlier came and said hello to Hendrik. Hendrik introduced me to Godlier. When the music started, Godlier asked Hendrik, "May I invite Mei for a dance?" Hendrik nodded. After the song, Godlier and I returned to the entrance where we first stood, but Hendrik was not there; he had gone back to the old seat at the back where we always sat. He did not look at us and was leisurely smoking. Godlier was still interested and asked for another dance. I had wanted to dance with him since I had come to the dance hall, as he was an even better dancer than Hendrik. However, Hendrik was a good match for me. He was more gentle, humble, and intellectual. Even when we did not dance, we got along well. He was humorous, which I enjoyed. When we danced together, his sweating forehead shines a bit. When he was excited, his eyes lit up and were energised. Godlier was younger than Hendrik and more direct. He said, "You are an excellent dance partner, how come I've never seen you before?" I just shrugged. Then he asked, "Can I have your phone number? I will take you to other places where we can dance".

After a few dances, Godlier took me back to my seat. He chatted with Hendrik for a short time, then left. Hendrik, in his normal friendly tone said, "Godlier loves dancing. He has been coming here for over for over a decade now".

I was happy that night. Hendrik and I were gentler whilst dancing, not trying to be fancy. But with Godlier, he pointed out some weakness of my dancing. I went to dance to enjoy, to relax, and get exercise. Of course, I loved the graceful movements, and I was willing to improve my dancing skills.

It was late when I got back home, but surprisingly, my phone rang. It was Godlier. I was not expecting this. He said with enthusiasm "Mei, you are a good dancer, but I can help you improve even more. We should go to where real dancers go, not to the social dance hall. There are no good dancers there". I thought why not, Hendrik seems to not have any real interest in a relationship. So I agreed, and we went to different venues, especially for tango, which I adore.

I danced a lot with Godlier, and he phoned often. I decided I would not go to the social dance hall to meet Hendrik. In the past I felt such harmony when together we enjoyed each other, but we were like just friends without dating. I was confused by his interest but not furthering it. Now, Godlier's attention made me feel good. One day, Godlier invited me to go to the house of a friend, Katrina, to dance. It was a Saturday night, so I dressed up. When he saw me, his eyes sparkled, "My God, you are beautiful and sexy".

"Well, it's the weekend and we are going dancing so why not dress up. Besides, you also look nice in your check shirt and jeans… you have a nice body and you look good in anything". Godlier beamed, gave me his arm, and said, "Come. We go to the cake shop to buy cake". At the shop, Godlier chose five apple pies, five black forest cakes, and five strawberry cream cakes. I asked him in surprise, "So many, how can we consume all of this?" Godlier laughed and said, "Aren't we going to dance? With all the exercise, we can eat as much as we want. And even if we don't finish it all, we can share it with friends.

I regretted that I did not bring a gift, and was surprised by Godlier's generosity to his friends. Usually he goes to this place to teach dancing on a voluntarily basis, and now he also bought all these cakes for his friends. He said to me, "Baby, this is an investment for when I'm old. You need to use your heart to make friends. I met Katrina at a dance, about five years ago. Katrina is a good person, and her family is very nice. I teach her and her two daughters and son to dance. I will spend a happy afternoon with her and her family. I hope to keep this friendship forever. You need friends who have a common interest in your life".

After the dance at Katrina's, Godlier insisted on taking me home. I had not had such nice attention from men for a long time. I liked being with him. I accepted his lift.

My home did not have much furniture. I liked the open space for Tantan to play, and for me to dance. When I was recovering after the cancer and treatments, my parents came from China to take care of my son. It was wonderful hearing my parent's voice, caring and talking to Tantan, and his giggling with joy. Tantan often rode his small bicycle around this empty home, screaming and shouting with happiness. I enjoyed what the emptiness brings. It also gave me a room to be quiet and on my own for a bit.

As it has been two years since I had my surgery, my parents returned to China. I must take up my responsibilities. With them gone, the house is too still. The emptiness too empty, too quiet. After the final break up with Yun, my soul and body are as empty as the house. I am lonely. When Godlier comes in, he fills my living room. I pour two glasses of wine and put on a waltz. Both my heart and body have a long hidden desire. I feel there is strength, deep within, that is trying to break through.

The slow waltz is gentle. I enjoy Godlier's hand that supports my waist and gives direction for the movement. I'm comfortable, slowly melting. I need time to overcome both the emotional and mental barrier. He moves closer, holding me tighter. I like it. His breath gentle in my ear, "Baby, you always look nice, but now you are so sexy and pretty. Do you like this?" I nod in his arms.

He continues, "I like you very much, and want to make you happy. When we first met, I thought you looked a bit plain but after the second look, I became attracted to you. After chatting with you, I found you to be so interesting. Now, I hold you in this embrace and my feelings for you are strong. You are the woman I don't want to lose. Since the first time I danced with you, I don't want to lose you".

Godlier's words are very nice, I am pleased. But I am not sure of myself. Because my German is not much beyond conversational, I miss many of the nuances of the customs and culture. Often, I feel at a disadvantage, and do not understand many of the German jokes. My Chinese customs are of no use. Although they complement me on my 'baby German', it is inferior to their normal mother tongue. Now Godlier say these things, and I am unable to appraise the real intention behind the words.

In China, when I was thirteen or fourteen, my breasts were bigger than my girlfriends. Every morning, I squashed my breasts into a tight bra to try to flatten them before going to school. Later, when at University, my first boyfriend complained that my breasts were too big, not like a virgin's. I was hurt and felt inferior. A decade later, China had changed and Chinese men started to appreciate bigger breasts and more backside. There were products on the market to make these look bigger. When I arrived in Germany, I realised that compared to German women, my breasts and bottom were about average. But I learnt that for German men, Asian girls have a mysterious lure. I have always received plenty of appreciation from German men.

I am unsure about this. I wonder if he really means that he does not want to lose me. I am a little unsettled. I wonder if I should be upset, or happy. I seemed to not be able to accept it naturally like most German females do, to naturally enjoy the situation and let my body enjoy it. I know though, that I would be unhappy if he did not want to hold me.

With the rhythm of the music, he moves his hand down in a testing way to my backside. Because I am confused, I ask him, "Do you have a sexual partner?"

"Yes, I do." He does not hesitate in replying and continues, "I have a permanent partner... There was a time I had two at the same time".

I am greatly relieved. I do not want him to have strong feelings for me just because he had no other woman.

I have different feelings for Hendrik than Godlier. My feelings for Hendrik are strong, and I hope that he has the same feelings towards me. With Godlier, I enjoy being with him, but I don't have strong feelings for him. It does not matter that Godlier has other women, he tries to make me happy – this is enough. I have no burdens. Godlier continues his sweet words, "Baby, these days I only think of you, I want to know you more".

Godlier has no hurry. "With your dancing, you should straighten up your back. Lift your butt up, tuck in your belly, don't cling to me, keep your distance. Remember, when you dance you need to be responsible for your own balance".

I laugh, mainly to cover my embarrassment. When I am dancing, I always collapse my body on Godlier to save my energy; it's also because my centre of gravity is not as stable as it used to be. I am not fit enough. But now, Godlier is being strict. He has danced competitive dancing for a long time, and I feel my ability is poor. I feel proud of his, and shamed about mine.

I do not know when was it; we both ended up on the lounge. Nor for how long we were there. With my shirt undone, he felt my scar and exclaimed, "What is this?" I was embarrassed and did not know what to say. I did not want to tell him I had cancer. Godlier's hand moved around with concern, "Mei, this a long scar, what is it?"

I could not see his face in the darkened room. I held my breath and said, "I had cancer. I had operations two years ago".

His voice changed marginally, "What kind of cancer?"

"Rectal Cancer... Does this matter to you?"

"Doesn't matter to me. But it must be a disaster for you, and difficult to face".

Godlier's kisses covered my ears and neck. His two hands did not stop either. But he did not get erect. I had never encountered such a situation and felt confusion.

Godlier sensed my embarrassment. He said in a calm voice, "Don't let this make you feel uncomfortable. Do not worry about me. I am always like this. Sometimes I make love for myself, sometimes I make love just for the woman". I was stunned that he seemed to have no real sexual interest in me. Was it the scar, the cancer, or was it that he was not interested in me sexually? I could not tell. I tried, but without success. I knew my body was waking up – I smelt the pure essence of the naturally brewed wine from the banks of Rhine River; I felt the velvet-smooth olive oil that came from mountains of Italy. Gradually, I became a water lily in Monet's painting, while I was also the Chinese lotus flower that emerged from the mud to shine from the oil painting, *Lotus Water Lily*. I want love, I want love ... I want love, I want to be alive....

Since that night, Godlier has not called. I hope to get calls from him because I am embarrassed. I asked myself why, and knew I had no real deep feelings for him. Our relationship was not one of harmony like the one with Hendrik. I simply like Godlier and enjoy dancing with him. Godlier only likes me as well in that way. It is normal that Godlier has less interest in me and is afraid of my body. How could I expect him to be enthusiastic?

It took me a lot of time and effort to allow myself be get to this point. I have been terrified of contact with a man. I told myself that my relationship with Godlier was one where I was testing myself. I am not ready to love again. I need to regain my confidence.

I left a message on Godlier's phone, "Hi Godlier, I thank you. I will be taking my son back to China for a while. I will remember your dance lessons forever. Goodbye".

I will not forget him because he showed me that I am now ready to open my body up to others. I will remember his body rhythm and dancing forever, I will remember his words of encouragement.

MOVEMENT UNDER THE WAIST

(a term suggesting the controlled movement below the waist, (bottom, feet, etc.) when dancing.

After I went back to China, I did not care if Yun had affairs with other women or my sister. I said to myself, "Let it go, let it go, let them both go. Be yourself". I don't do yoga, but I meditate a few minutes every day to remind myself to let it go, and to know who I am.

Dance filled my life in Berlin, so when I arrived back in Beijing, I searched out an old business card of one of my past dance teachers. I called her office and asked her to introduce me to a couple of dance teachers.

In the spring of 2003, the unexpected SARS virus broke out, and it was especially bad in China. The seasons seemed to be upside down, people on the streets were covered with many layers of masks. They covered themselves for the whole day. Everyone was in a panic.

I, like the other millions of people, hid from the news. I said goodbye to the fresh air of Berlin, capital city of Germany, and took my three-year-old son back to Beijing, the capital city of China. I walked the streets of Beijing during the day. I passed people who were covered from head to toe. I tried to remain unconscious of the disaster and enjoyed being back in my motherland. I sent my son to a temporary childcare centre in Beijing. Later, I heard that two kids in that care centre were sick, but I continued to send my son there.

In the spring of 2003, I have no privacy in my home at Beijing. The apartment has smooth clean floors, a floor to ceiling window in one of the walls. It is tiny, with only one bedroom, and without much furniture. It does not have an American style open kitchen but I do not bother to cook. The house has no cooking aromas. I do have a professional home dancehall. The two dance teachers arrive. I treat them with German chocolates. I do not know if they brought SARS germs with them. Every night I have lessons, I enjoy the lessons but expect disasters anytime.

I admired the couple who were my dance teachers. The male teacher had a fine body-shape for dancing. He always wore a dark coloured suite. The thing that grabbed my attention were the shoes he wore. They were old but always shiny and well-polished. The female teacher was different. Every day, a different dress. She matched these with different coloured scarves and tops. Her dresses were not flamboyant, but the different look every day was nice. She told me that her dresses were reasonably priced because she knew where to get them. "Perhaps, some time I will show you where to find them?"

I asked them if they had been to Europe. They replied with sad smiles that they had not. They went on to say that they would like to go to Blackpool in England to attend the Latin Dance competition. "This would be the highlight of my life", said the man with a distant smile.

On the 18th April 2003, a Friday, I left Tantan in Beijing and I went back to Berlin. In Berlin, I realised just how bad the SARS virus was in Asia. Previously, after I returned to Berlin, I would go to my various friends' places for breakfast to catch up on their news. But now they all refused, saying, "Sorry, but you just came back from China, we are afraid that you will pass the SARS germs onto our children". A few of my girlfriends' kids were younger than Tantan. As much as I would have liked to see them, I kept away. It seemed that this SARS was very severe, and some even said that it could be caught through using a phone that a sufferer had used.

On Saturday, before the shops opened, I covered myself and went shopping to stock up on groceries. Then I stayed home for a few days, not going out. One day I was cleaning my house with the radio on, listening to a jazz station. Although an only jazz music station, it did have news bulletins, and it gave a breaking report about the SARS epidemic in China. It seemed that many of the Chinese officials had been kicked out of their jobs. It went on to say that the virus was expanding. This was a real worry. I did not want to hear more and so I took out some old jazz CDs to listen to; Louis Armstrong, Duke Ellington and his Big Band. I liked most of the music of that period. Listening to it, I realised that over the years my taste had changed.

It was about a week later that I got Tantan out of China and back to Germany. This was a real escape, as apparently many wanted to get on the plane. Even Yun was denied a seat and could not accompany his young son. The flight was not direct, so I had to catch the train from Berlin to Frankfurt to pick him up. He was wearing a big white mask. The childcare centre that Tantan goes to in Berlin told me to have Tantan checked out by a doctor before they would readmit him. Only when the result showed that he was okay, they welcomed him back. A month later, my friends, one by one, called, apologised, and issued invites. When I arrived at these various friends' home, the first thing I did was to sing the classic song of Billie Holiday, *You've Changed*, "You've changed, now all are finished." I laughed loudly. "You've changed, you don't want me and Tantan, but we are not finished, we are both fine".

A week after I returned to Berlin, and with no signs of fever or a cough, I felt I could go dancing. I had not seen Hendrik for almost two months. When he saw me, I could tell he was excited. He tried not to make this obvious but I could feel it. I hoped our reunion led to more than the last time. I was apprehensive, even though I thought we both had feelings for each other. He took me onto the dance floor, where we danced to a few songs. After these, he was a bit more relaxed, "Hey, Mei, you're here. I am relieved now I know you are safe. I heard that SARS is everywhere in China. Good you are in Germany, it's safe here". Hendrik held me tighter than before. I felt a bit guilty because of Godlier. I leaned my head onto his chest; we were in harmony. In Hendrik's hug, I suddenly had the thought to myself, "If I told you that I was in Beijing a week ago, would you be terrified?" Instead I said, "I have many relatives there and so I stayed at home and listened to jazz to make myself feel better".

He laughed, "Jazz… when I worked in Japan I had a Japanese colleague who was fond of jazz. He gave me a book about two Japanese super jazz fans, Makoto Wada, and Haruki Murakami. One is a painter, the other a novelist. I didn't understand the novelist because he wrote in

Japanese. But the painter painted the jazz Player extremely well. It's very interesting... he lent me a lot of jazz CDs".

We talked and went back to our seats. We were still talking about jazz. I said, "It's well known that jazz is a mixture of different music. It is the hot sunlight of West Africa, while it's also the romantic spirit of France. It's a magic mix with the rebellious spirit from the black people. However, Isadora Duncan, who was the doyen of Contemporary Dance, despised Ball Room Dancing. She thought that the traditional waltz, Mazuka Dance, and small step, are not healthy, they are too emotional. She thought good American dancers could not feature in international ballet because their legs were too long, their bodies were too strong, they loved freedom so much, they were not graceful enough. Because of this, her dance is of a creative free style, she discarded the restrictions of the old and became a pioneer of creative dance." I sipped my drink, saw the shinning eyes of Hendrik.

And listen to me. I had forgotten how annoyed I felt when I heard Germans say the word *aber* (which I used), which means 'but'. At that moment, my German took a leap forward. I am so proud of my talking and prolonged the *aber* pronunciation on purpose. "Ms. Duncan, she's an old time pioneer, and looked down upon jazz. I think she was being shallow. Ms. Duncan thought that jazz was music for wild people. She said it is immature and cute. She called on American composers to leave this medium. Jazz does not involve rhythm under the waist, nor does it allow for a good shake action, which is so sexy. She didn't want the black people's dance influence, which she thought contains too much lust. But history is not to be stopped, Duncan passed away in 1927 in a car accident. 1927 is the year where America embraced jazz.

During World War Two, the American soldiers took jazz to Europe. Fifty years later, jazz lost a bit of popularity in America. Thereafter, it rocketed up again. I don't think Ms. Duncan would have expected this for America... Haha".

Coincidently, right then, the band played a jazz rhythm. Hendrik leaned towards to me and spoke into my ear "Honoured lady, do you want some movement under the waist?" We looked at each other and smiled as we headed to the dance floor and danced the Sumba.

This night we are tight with each other again. Godlier is nowhere to be seen. I do not want to think of that interlude with Godlier. I do not want to think that Hendrik may have had other women in that time. "Mei, I have been in this dance hall for over twenty years. I have met many women, some come, some gone, some married, some divorced, and then returned. Ha ha… you should remember my words, I will always be here".

What does Hendrik mean? He won't go? He doesn't want to get married again? If so, then why did he want a divorce? He wants this dance hall as his eternal home? Did he come here when he was married to his Korean wife? No, it seems not, because he said, it is worth it to have his son.

After we spoke about jazz, after the dance, we went to a bar called the A-Train, which was well known as a jazz venue. When East and West Berlin were separated by the wall, two famous jazz bars popped up, one in East Berlin, the other in West Berlin. The one in the west, The A-Train, is close to my place, so naturally we went to that one.

Walking along a narrow road, from the dance hall, it only takes around ten minutes to walk there. The jazz bar is small, only around a hundred square metres, but it is always packed. The bar area is small, a small dance floor, and the lights above the dance floor are colourful, like a party. The patrons here are different from those of the social dance hall, with many international tourists as well. If you want a table, it is always best to pre-book. Hendrik and I had not booked and just arrived.

It is unusual to go to a jazz venue by yourself. Most of the time a few friends go together. With Hendrik in the bar, the jazz was great, but it is our time together that I remember with the most fondness. Why? Because this jazz bar is very crowded, it's hard to find a quiet space. When I listen to jazz, I prefer to sit in a quiet space and appreciate the music, and what it evokes in me. I don't know if other people get the same feelings as I do. When on my own, once the performance is finished, and when I go home by myself, I normally feel melancholic, and often feel homesick. Every time, when Hendrik and I say goodbye to each other, Hendrik calls a taxi for me. If the weather is good, I will wave my hand and stop him from calling one. I don't even want him to send me home. I would rather go home by myself late at night, then I can appreciate the feelings within and my homesickness.

I KEEP AWAY FROM HENDRIK

I was very busy every day. I had no time to be worried or feel hopeless. The SARS epidemic in China dominated my thoughts, even though so far away. In 2002, I advocated for the first youth art festival between Germany and China in Berlin. The Mayor of Berlin, Herr Wolvelake, was the honoured chairman. We invited over 400 young Chinese and German artists to come to Berlin. We met at a venue, with a large hall, where we dined together, boarded there, practice the programmes there, and practiced on the stage. By doing so, we formed deep friendships. We planned to meet again next year in Beijing where it was to be returned. In 2003, the Mayor of Berlin, Herr Wolvelake, was again to be the chairman for the second art festival between China and Germany. But the sudden attack of SARS ruined it. Both the Chinese and German art groups cancelled. But one group did not. This was the Choir of the high school attached to Shanghai's Tongji University. They insisted on going to Berlin. More appreciated though, was a German group who insisted that this Chinese choir come. They were the jazz band of Jonalist Buzbaher high school. They did not believe that all Chinese people had the SARS virus, and so they wanted to support the Chinese group.

Some wondered if the setup costs were too great for only two groups. I had simply to support these two groups which were so determined to get to know each other. I was determined to have an event in Berlin to show support for the Chinese with their battle with SARS.

I was excited. Because of my excitement, I was creative, and for the next two months, I, together with a few work colleagues, performed miracles to make it happen. To hold this performance there were three elements: place, programs, and audiences. The Berlin World Culture Palace (Haus Der Kulturen Der Welt) is a symbol of multiculturalism in Berlin. The architecture was highly praised by the big smiling American president Carter. There are large fountains, surrounded by green parkland. The parkland adjoins the tranquil Spree River. I felt that because the Berlin World Culture Palace is a landmark of Berlin, if our performance could be held there it would benefit both, the young German and Chinese performers, as well as the audience. They would all have a wonderful experience. We got the palace through my persistent efforts. The first round was a request in writing. Their reply stated that there is already an arrangement on the day of 20th July. But I did not give up. Through an internal contact, I knew the arrangement for that day was for an annual concert. Luckily, in 2003 the show was cancelled. I was still hopeful. I started my second round of liaison, again in writing. I wrote in German, and lavishly praised the friendship between Germany and China. I listed the importance of the Chinese battle against SARS, and how it would be good for China's morale. They replied that they will try to offer it and went on to inform that the rent and technician fees would be very expensive, around 7000 Euro. In the third and fourth rounds of communication, I kept stressing how meaningful the festival would be to both groups. In the end, the Berlin World Culture Palace organisers reduced the price to 3000 Euro and designated it as 'for the consideration of political and culture purpose'.

An attractive programme was also very important as well. My colleagues and I decided to open the festival with the Chinese choir, where they were to perform a beautiful melodic piece. In between, there were to be dance programmes. The finale was to be the German Jazz band, with the hope of raising the atmosphere to a crescendo. However, where could I find dancers?

The news of holding the art festival in Berlin for Chinese support against SARS spread quickly. Some Chinese people in China were heartened and came for the performance. There also were six boys and six girl students who came from Tibet, who wanted to perform a Tibetan cultural dance.

The dance they wanted to perform was from the Han people of China and was called *Solider Brother*. But it was hard to find the traditional costume of the Han. To perform the dance of *Solider Brother*, we needed stage props and costumes. I made over a hundred phone calls but finally ordered twelve sets from China, and entrusted friends to urgently send them from Beijing to Shanghai – then we got the Shanghai group to bring them to Berlin. We used German props for the rest.

Knowing dance as well as I do, especially after that pair of teachers in Beijing, I knew that there was not much communication between the Chinese Latin dance community and the European. So, after I got back to Berlin, I wrote a letter to the Chairman of Berlin Dance Association to introduce myself. He and his wife were enthusiastic to encourage me. This happened at the time of the *5th World Youth National Standard Dance and Latin Dance Competition* held in Berlin. They invited me as an honoured guest to attend. They told me the story about Lisa and Daniel, who were the champions of this competition – in order to get the best possible partner, Daniel left his Australian home and family, at only fourteen years of age. He went to Berlin to live and train, and to collaborate with Lisa. The pair obviously succeeded and became the champions. When I saw the pair dance, they were amazingly active and energetic. I felt so moved that I invited them to performance at our art festival to support China against SARS. Lisa and Daniel agreed to take time from their busy international dance schedule and dance at the festival.

My old friend, the Principal of the Art School Atrium Berlin, Mr. Link, also appointed the famous contemporary dance director, Mr. Keith, to lead a team named *Quick as a flash* to perform at the festival as well.

So we had Chinese National style dance, German Contemporary dance, standard dance, where these different styles of dance were arranged for free to support the festival.

I was under immense pressure during the day preparing for the event. I had no energy or time to dance with Hendrik at night. I invited Hendrik for dinner and said, "You always pay for my drinks so tonight I will pay for dinner. Please choose a nice restaurant". Without hesitation, he chose the *Oyster Restaurant*. He said he lived nearby. That area is the most affluent area in Berlin. House prices in that area are sky-high. However, average people also lived within the area.

As the name suggested, they specialised in oysters and seafood. The staff were all highly trained, standing with upright posture and with good manners, moving about with grace. You can tell a restaurant level from their service level, and I was happy to pay an upmarket price for good food and service. I wanted to enjoy the night with Hendrik.

But it seemed that he did not intend to eat a big meal. He insisted we order only the oyster soup. He said, "It will be enough". I didn't mind spending big money for a top restaurant meal and a good ambience. I silently sighed. I really wanted to spoil him and show my appreciation. I felt I needed more than just a bowl of soup. After all, to be in such a fine restaurant, and not derive its full offering seemed sacrilegious, so I also ordered the striped bass with a white wine sauce for my main meal. Because it was seafood, I ordered a glass of white wine.

In Germany, most seafood restaurants already place a bottle of wine on the table. This meant we had two bottles! I also got a bottle of spring water. As soon as we poured our drinks, I told Hendrik of my involvement in the show I was putting on. As I talked, I realised how excited I was. "You know the dancer, Duncan? I mentioned her once before…, people think she was the originator of contemporary dance. She thought her dance was influenced by her grandmother. Apparently, her grandmother migrated to America from Ireland. Missing Ireland, she sang Irish songs, and danced various jigs. These jigs the grandmother danced encompassed the spirit of the frontiersman, and the war against the Native American Indian people. Later, Duncan's grandfather returned from the civil war, where he sang the popular songs of the soldiers. The grandmother sang with him. Duncan learnt the ethos of these modern songs and dances from her grandmother, and created her own dance. You see, any type of dance contains the national spiritual and culture".

Hendrik listened in silence with a smile.

When our soup arrived, my eyes widened in shock. The waiter was holding a tureen that was as big as a bucket. He returned with two bowls that one could have a small bath in. When he returned the third time, it was with a large French baguette, cut it into pieces, with two kinds of butter, and a plate of green-olives without pips. I was fascinated and watched with apprehension. When Hendrik saw my amazement, with a wry smile he said to the waiter, "Take plenty of time to serve the main meal, let the lady digest her soup first". Then he looked at me with a questioning gleam. I nodded my head happily in defeat. Yet, Hendrik did not scoff.

The waiter replied, "Of course, sir. Waiting for your call".

The soup had a lovely velvety sheen and was garnished with a few sprigs of green spring onion. I daintily placed my spoon into the soup and focused on the flavour. It was so fresh. "Ahhhaaa, wonderful". Because the bowl was so large this was going to take time. Hendrik put a piece of bread on my plate. I chose the same spread as Hendrik used to spread on the bread. The flavour of the spread was almost the same as the soup; it was just a bit salty. Then I had a green olive; everything matched perfectly. Hendrik relished my enjoyment, and asked, "Do you like it here?" I nodded my head "It's incredible, such a good choice... I have passed this place a few times and never thought of coming in and dinning here". I ate in silence for a bit before saying, "Now, let me tell you about the contemporary dance".

I could see that Hendrik's eyes were shining, "Please do, I would love to hear about it".

"But why is there contemporary dance? I think the existence of contemporary dance is because of the contemporary spirit. The reason for the contemporary dance is to have worldwide unity. Once there is connection, the connection would melt into the arts. The reason why Pina Bausch of German was successful was because her contemporary dance expressed the common topic of this world. She was born in 1940, that is the Second World War period. Therefore, childhood and death, memory and forget became a non-forgettable topic in her dance. Pina Bausch said about contemporary, "I dance because I feel sad, I dance against the fear. I care about why people move, but not how people move".

After this I stopped, I sipped my wine, looked at Hendrik, then I encouraged myself. I felt a little bit nervous, because I didn't know if Hendrik would care about what I am going to say next, "Actually, I don't like to dance socially too much. I don't really care about the appointed movement in Chinese National dance, but I care about the national culture meaning of the movement. I am thinking of the races who created the dance while I am dancing. Or, when I dance Disco, or a piece of contemporary dance, I always soak myself in the cultural feelings. I like to express my feelings freely. These feelings are not in the social dance. No matter when I am dancing, in my university days or at present, the most joyful times springs from the attitude of my partner. If he is enjoying himself, then I am more likely to enjoy myself, irrespective of the dance".

Hendrik listened with polite interest, nodding his head every so often. His smile was warm, which comforted my heart. His arm was relaxed over the back of my chair. I could not help but smile as well. How foolish I was just now by telling him I did not actually like social dancing, and that I only went there to push away the loneliness so I could move on with my life. But life is funny as sometimes we do the wrong things for the right reason, and I ended up liking Hendrik, and like dancing with him. Of course, Hendrik seemed happy. I was joyful that I could express myself as I did. I continued, "Out of national dance and contemporary dance or ballet, I prefer contemporary the most. In China, we have contemporary dance as well. I admire Pina Bausch. She worked for the conservative theatre of Wuppertal, but she didn't change her method to suite the establishment – she did it her way.

In the thirty years there, she created the most unique work that no other theatre could emulate. The creativity that she got from her performers was outstanding. Not only that, the visual effects were really special. Yet, the audiences of the Wuppertal were used to classic ballet. They hated it, and rallied against her. When she sat at the last row to watch her own show, the audience spat on her, and called out insults to her. They wanted her to get out immediately from the Wuppertal. It was only many years later, when that old batch were replaced with a younger audience that the appreciation came. Now, when there is a Pina Bausch performance, huge audiences attend. They come from all over the world to fill the Wuppertal theatre. Her dance is pure heart, of dirty bodies, flowers on the stage, natural green foliage, real mud, and rubbish. This confronted many".

As I talked, I had tears in my eyes, but I was too moved to wipe them away. Hendrik is not usually emotive, but he appreciated my emotion well. He placed his arm on my shoulder. Because of this inspired story, I hardly noticed the flavours of my main meal. At that moment when taking a break from talking, he spooned ice cream into my mouth. The contrast of cool and flavour was fresh. I saw the appreciation and enjoyment in his eyes.

He treated me so gently, as if I was a sad child. I cried and laughed.

After the dinner, we held onto each other and wandered around. We walked from the Olive ground, passed the Lenin precinct, until we arrived at Marquis Road, and arrived at Halensee Lake. We were to walk around the lake, but half way around we found the path blocked by houses. We remembered there was an outcry in Berlin about the rich people being able to build there. By doing so, they removed the right for the public to walk around the lake. Apparently, later, the government regretted the move but by then it was too late. This happened a long time ago, but Hendrik and I still criticised the government, the property company, and the owners who lived in those luxury houses.

That night, finally, Hendrik said he would like to accompany me home. We enjoyed the walk. As we had not danced, the exercise was good. When we arrived at the front of my building, I felt Hendrik hesitate. I also felt a bit awkward. Compare to the ease of Godlier, I could not relax myself at that moment. Nor could I take the next step. Hendrik looked up at the building in the dim light, a slight smile on his face. I bit my lips and mumbled, "Well, thanks for walking me home. It is late and I still have some work to do. I will invite you in for coffee another time." It seemed that we agreed, as he said he didn't intend to go inside. I controlled my emotions and in a friendly tone asked Hendrik if he would like to attend the art show with me. I really wanted him to come. I hoped he could bring some of his friends as well. But because I am the organiser, I did not know why it was so hard for me to express my hope for his attendance.

WORLD CULTURE PALACE OF BERLIN, 20TH JULY 2003 NIGHT

It was a wonderful night, and here I briefly describe it. The school choir of the Tongji University was beautiful, their combined voice was clean and in harmony. When the Han dancers started, their clothes grabbed the attention of the audience. Although there were only two performers from the *Quick as Flash* Super Contemporary Dance Group of Berlin, they performed with fluidity, expressing the conflict, struggle and pain of people's internal turmoil.

The dancing of Lisa and Daniel was the highlight for most of the Chinese audience.

I had arranged the Jazz band to perform at the end. Everyone went crazy for them, and the applause went on for a long time. Then for the finale, I had the school choir return to the stage and sing with the Jazz band to perform a Chinese version of the song *Jasmine*. The collaboration was stunning and had the audience on their feet applauding wildly.

The Chinese ambassador to Germany, Mr. Canrong Ma, made a passionate speech about the SARS epidemic in China. There were many distinguished guests, both Chinese and German, in the front seats, who later came to the back of the stage to offer their congratulations.

After the show, but whilst still on the stage, were all the young performers. Gifts were offered. First to the Chinese youths, then to the German. They were all nervous and shy as the audience clapped. Mr. Victor, who was the responsible person for organising the German Youth Art Festival, also said a few words to the audience and performers, where he spoke about the support of the German people for the Chinese people in this time of difficulty. He then made it a bit lighter when he spoke of his desire for more Chinese dishes. This made everyone laugh.

He congratulated all the students for their rich talent. He finished off by saying that there would be a return challenge in China next year. Everyone cheered.

The broadcast team of CCTV came to Berlin to film the performance and the speeches, and the next day, CCTV 4 broadcasted it on the news.

It was only ten months later, when the Jazz Band of Bucibaher middle school visited China led by the principal. They became the first German Student Art group to visit China, and it was under my organisation. This was the start of a long and traditional relationship between the schools.

I didn't see Hendrik in the hall. I was disappointed because it seemed that he did not care about my work – what I had put my heart and soul into. "He may not really care that I am Chinese… He only dances with me because I am a good dancer… his feelings for me are ambiguous". I was depressed afterwards, when I should have been euphoric. Once again I decided not go to the social dance hall any more, to forget him.

I WANT GO BACK TO CHINA

One night, a month later, at the beginning of autumn, I was in a pub with a few friends, when a song was played that was a favourite of Hendrik's and mine that we danced to. Overwhelmed with emotion, I bid my friends goodbye and rushed to the dance hall. Hendrik was sitting at a table towards the front. He sat with a woman. I passed by his table so he could see me as I went to the back table where we usually sat. I sat down and waited.

A long time passed, and Hendrik did not come. Nor did he dance with the woman. I walked back to his table, nodded to the lady, and invited Hendrik to dance. The woman smiled and indicated that it was okay for Hendrik to dance with me. He looked at me with a wide smile that held no embarrassment. His voice was his normal calm when he said, "Mei, I can't dance with you tonight".

"Why?... Remember the rule where a male must not refuse a woman's invitation. I would like to dance with you for one song".

"Not tonight".

I was flustered and turned back to the lady, "If you don't mind, I just want to dance with him for one song".

The lady nodded a slight nod and said, "I don't mind, but it's his decision".

I looked at Hendrik, but he stubbornly said the same thing, "Not tonight Mei, maybe next time".

His smile remained in place but he stopped looking at me. He just stared ahead. I stood beside the table for a few seconds, not knowing what to do. Then I walked out of the dance hall without a backward glance.

I had given my phone number to Hendrik, but I knew he would not call me. However, the next day there was a message on my phone, "Mei, congratulations. Your show was wonderful. I was sitting upstairs, you may not have seen me. Since it has been over a month that you didn't come to the dance hall, I didn't expect to see you again. Please remember, I would be there forever. Next time, when you come, we could have a chance to dance together".

I never returned to Berlin Social Dance Hall.

Since then, I have been back to China often. There was one time when I watched a play of *Da Guo and Ming Cai*. I almost threw my dinner bowl on the floor. Da Guo looked so much like Hendrik. His head, his demeanour, the only difference was that Guo spoke Chinese and Hendrik spoke German. Guo's eyes were black and Hendrik's grey-blue. I liked the show of *Da Guo and Ming Cai*, but was saddened. It seemed that my eyes were watching but my brain was thinking of Hendrik. Halfway through I walked out miserable. I knew on the stage it was Da Guo and Ming Cai. In reality, Hendrik was my dance partner. On the stage Da Guo was upset with Ming Cai, but in reality, Hendrik was never upset with me. He is a gentle and peaceful man.

I must let him go. As the weeks passed I was better, but he still came to my mind. Hendrik had that experience with his Asian wife. When he met her, he was young, she was exciting and creative. He must have loved her. They had a son. A decade after they divorced; he said with a sigh, "My wife even beat me sometimes". As an Asian girl, when I heard the story, I felt embarrassed.

Hendrik is now cautious, too cautious. It's impossible for me to ask Hendrik directly. I am still an Asian woman, it is against our culture. Even though I have thought about asking him over hundreds time, it's hard for me to ask him directly. Although I have strong feelings for him, I try to understand this from a rational point. Am I ready? Can I have new love?

After the storms of my life, I try to be stronger and firmer than before, but sometimes, still like a teenager, I am nervous, which is hard to overcome. I tell myself that I won't hold romantic aspirations like before, I won't belittle myself, I won't treat a handsome German like a prince any more. I start to criticise Germany and myself. I must stop. After all, Germany is now in my blood, but it is hard for me to fall in love with a German man so easily.

I thought about it over and over again. I was like the character of Daiyu Lin in the Chinese novel *Red Building Dream*. I turned around and locked myself up.

I did not dance with Hendrik anymore. One night I dreamt that the 'God of Death' came to invite me to dance. He was very gentle. All the barriers of death were removed. The barriers between lovers, the distance between friends, and misunderstanding from parents … I allowed him to take my arm and placed it on his shoulder. I held him tight. I looked directly into his eyes and asked him to take me away.

Most days I am confused. Most nights I have the nightmare. I have parents, a three-year-old son. I just started a new job and feel that life started again, the cancer, and Yun, my sister…… should I go with the Angel of Death? I do not want to die. Please God of Death, take me and dance, never stop, take me back to China to dance. Unconsciously, I treat the God of Death like a close friend.

When I wake up from the stranglehold of the dream, I feel stronger and more in control. I aspired to love, but I am not sure if I am ready to fall in love again in Germany. Nevertheless, I do want to go back to China again for a time. I like walking between China and Germany.

PIANO AND LOVE

I married Jim, I divorced Jim. With the passage of time some things cannot be retrieved, we need to forget and move on. However, I kept thinking, what am I thinking? Jim came to hospital to visit me; after he had gone, I recalled his voice. It was in low tones, but the order is clear, Tantan, flowers, book...... actually I hoped he would say that he will play the piano for me. But he didn't.

Did I love Jim or did I love the fact that Jim played the piano? My generation of Chinese seldom play the piano. When I was in university in China, Richard Clayderman's piano pieces were broadcasted all the time. It seemed that there was only one *L V Beethoven Für Elise* piano music. I appreciated this music, I gained appreciation of Johann Sebastian Bach; I liked Bach more.

When I arrived in Germany, I hoped that the man who would fall in love with me would play the piano. At that time, I worked hard. It was an afternoon in 1990, the sunlight was brilliant and the German houses under the blue sky and white cloud were beautiful. Wearing a white shirt, black skirt and a denim coat, I went to a Chinese restaurant where I worked part-time. It was then I met Matiyas.

Matiyas came from Munster to do his Doctorate. After we got to know each other, he came to visit me. In my simple student apartment, we sat face-to-face drinking beer and chatting. Like all the other Germans, he asked me how long had I been in Germany. How did I come here? I wondered, would his next question be the one when I am asked as to when I will be going back to China? But Matiyas did not ask this question. He asked me what my major was. He asked what my parents did. Do I have any brothers or sisters? He told me that he has four brothers, he is the youngest.

Matiyas was not like other Germans, he was less arrogant. He was curious but not pushy. I felt comfortable with him. When he said, "It must be hard for you to live in Germany by yourself", suddenly I was nostalgic for China. In Germany, my life was so different. I worked in the Chinese restaurant just for one day a week. On that day, I washed so many cups, more than I had in all my life in China. I had a very good life in China but here I had to go and work to make my living. In fact, there was no another German person who had asked me this so directly. I opened my heart and told him of my loneliness.

Afterwards we went into the city, we walked across the gardens, which are opposite of Munster (old city). I told Matiyas excitedly that I saw the Chancellor of Germany Helmut Kohl. I told Matiyas that there were many people gathered in front of the Church. Suddenly, people moved aside to make way for the Chancellor as he came for the election campaign. I did not expect to see the Chancellor so easily. Even though there were not many people there, nor a stage to make a speech, the Chancellor stood opposite the church and made one. I asked Matiyas if he felt Kohl would become the next Chancellor of Germany. He replied, "That is not something that we need worry about. But he is likely to be the Chancellor of Germany for a soon to be united East and West Germany". We had arrived at the shops.

It seems that Matiyas cared about my German speaking, but not about whether Kohl would become the next Chancellor of Germany. He pointed to the goods in the shop windows and taught me German words, "That's a hat, this is a pair of pants". He taught me like one would teach a child. I nodded my head and could not help but laugh. I had been in Germany only for eight months and had already learnt many of these words.

Suddenly, Matiyas ran a bit further on before returning, "There was a cat there and I wanted to catch it for you to play with." He asked me what I would like to eat. I told him with a glee, "I like ice cream. German ice cream is so delicious. The colours are gorgeous". Matiyas laughed as well, he was happy like a child. "Sure, let's get ice cream.

We passed by a work site, with a Detour'sign. He laughed loudly and said, "But I want to go on this way, I don't want to go that way." I couldn't help but laugh, it was my happiest day since I arrived in

Germany. His laughter was infectious, and the sweet happy feelings of my past youth filled my heart.

Matiyas told me that his parents lived nearby. But he chose to study in Gottingen, which is far away. Now he came back to his parents and studied at Munster University to pursue his Doctorate. He suddenly stopped, turned around to me and asked, "It will take a few years to finish my Doctorate…will you wait for me?"

The question surprised me. What kind of question was this when I hardly knew him? Was he serious? Matiyas saw that I hesitated, thinking. He laughed, and to change the subject by saying his father had cancer, and only had six months left. I felt sorry to hear this. When Matiyas saw my sad face he turned around to look at me and said, "Don't worry, my father is a medical doctor, and so he understands his situation". He was so relaxed when he said this. I wondered if he was talking about his own father.

In the ice cream shop, I ordered a big ice cream with several flavours. Matiyas ordered a small one. We ate and chatted until it was time to go home. He went to the counter and paid the bill. He came back and said that we could go now. I said that I needed to pay my bill. He, with a smile, said that he had paid for us both. I said he should not do that, that I must pay my own. But Matiyas started to go out of the store and I had to follow him.

Outside, I said I wanted to give him the money for my ice cream. Matiyas said, "It's okay, I'm happy to pay for you." He then stopped walking and in a low tone asked, "Why? Is that how you do it in China?" I stopped as well, and replied in a voice that I hoped would not be confrontational, "In China, the men do pay for a lady. But I have learnt since being here that in Germany everyone pays his or her own bill… and so I must pay for mine". When I said this, I was self-conscious, and sure, my face was red. Of course I have to pay my own bill. Paying my own way is not natural, but I am careful about this in Germany. When I stood with these thoughts flashing through my mind, Matiyas finally understood and seemed a bit confused. For a moment, we stood there silently, face to face. He looked at me with apprehension, and in a shy way said, "But I like you. I want to".

I felt touched but embarrassed.

I asked Matiyas what he was doing in the restaurant that day. At first, it seemed that Matiyas did not understand my question, and was still embarrassed. "I saw you in the distance riding your bike. You looked so nice".

I replied, "I did not ask you this, I want to know what were you doing in the restaurant". He seemed to relax a bit, "I was about to tell you… I was looking for an apartment to rent as I just moved to this city. I have found one that I like. Originally, I only wanted to find a one bedroom apartment, but this one is a two bedrooms apartment, and I like it." Then, after a pause he said, "Would you like to live there with me? It's about 70 – 80 square metres". I stood and looked at him. "You ask the strangest questions". He laughed as if to cover it up and then whistled a happy tune.

The night was great fun, until we finally arrived at the front of my student accommodation. I suddenly felt the air was frozen between us. I did not know how to say goodnight. After an awkward pause, I thanked him and uttered a goodnight.

Quickly, he asked, "Can I come to see you again?".

I felt a panic and too quickly shook my head. Suddenly, there was disappointment on his face, his smile disappeared. He stood there for a while, perhaps expecting me to say something. But I didn't. Matiyas, with his head down, started to walk away. Then, he turned back to me and waved a hand. I stood there still, feeling bad.

How could I explain my mind to Matiyas? My German was not good enough and I did not want to say incorrect things. We had one night together of fun. I liked him, and I could feel he wanted to be close. But I was a student and came here to study. I also know that German men are attracted to Asian girls. I did not want to get caught up in that. I did not trust it. And, his strange questions…. Most Asian girls would normally be attracted to the openness of German men, their humour, and happy character. However, I was too proud to share my hard time with others. My self respect dictated that I had to spend my hardest time in Germany by myself.

When I worked my part-time job, I always thought of his laugh and easy way. He would say, "I am tall, you are petite". It was obvious that he was infatuated with me. I believe that Matiyas was less interested in

German girls who were almost the same height as him. At one stage I said I liked to listen to piano. He said that he has studied piano from when he was little, and that he can play for me every day in the future. The word 'everyday' had such a meaningful connotation that it hit my sensitive heart.

Matiyas did not come to see me again. Perhaps he did not come to Munster at all. Maybe his father passed away? Maybe his life had big changes, perhaps..., many perhapses, which became this poem that I called Deep Night:

>Deep night
>After the rain
>My feelings left pondering
>Never to stop
>the tranquil
>Bloom
>In the night
>You light up a match
>Relaxed and leisurely
>Spreading smoke
>But there was an arc
>Tight up you and me lightly
>Not know if the distance of heart
>Can be so close
>Make me feel sweet
>Please give me two suns
>One to irradiate me
>One to shine on my heart

STEPHAN

The longer I stayed in Germany, the more my character changed. Previously, I was persistent and stubborn. Now I was more open and relaxed. However, I longed for love and this affected my thoughts. Although many males appeared and disappeared in my life, I did not allow myself to fall in love with just anyone. I was also enjoying being single. I had plenty of friends, and classmates; we went skiing, swimming, dancing, or to concerts, and many other things. I often packed a bag and hitched-hiked to a remote and new city. I visited churches, enjoyed nature, and talked to people about their customs. But as I matured, I felt the stirrings of wanting to be with someone. There was no home for all the love within me. Occasionally, I even lost interest in life. It was at this stage Stephan came in my life. It was one evening, early spring in 1992. I went to the student shower block for a shower. I was in a good mood, wore a pink sweater, and a long skirt. Having forgotten my towel in my room, I hurried back to get it. When on the stairs, I saw an unknown male face watching me. He wore a tracksuit, having just returned from a run. I felt a bit strange, when he followed me up to my level. I knew all people on this floor but had never seen this man before.

When I entered my room, there he was hanging around the corridor, watching me without saying anything. I asked him who he's looking for. He shook his head, as if to say nobody. With my towel, I went back to the student bathrooms, which being in Germany were unisex. Privacy is gained by closing the door of the shower or toilet cubicle one was in. When I was about to close the shower door, there he was. Getting nervous, and angry, I asked him what was he doing. He shrugged shyly and said, "I saw you and wanted to get to know you. Would you please come and visit me?" He then told me the block and room number he was in.

I was sleepless that night. Unconsciously I felt disappointed, my intuition told me that we do not belong to each other. I do not know why, but my intuition is always right. I did not go out of my way to see Stephan, although I knew that he lived two levels below me. However, it was so long since I had had a relationship, my feelings seemed to be accumulating.

When Stephan saw me stand in front of his door, he let me in. He said he did not think I would visit him. He said the day when he followed me up the stairs, and to the shower block, that he could feel the cold in my voice, and that I slammed the door. He dressed casually, with a small scarf around his neck. In China, only girls wear scarfs, and at first, I was interested that men did that as well, without being feminine, but looking good.

At first, we were polite to each other and it a bit awkward. Anyway, we chatted. After some time I felt more comfortable with him. He also mentioned that he would help me to study German.

A week after, I was confused and now wanted to see him again. I erroneously thinking he was a man who could make me happy in loneliness while I was overseas.

I kept thinking about him, it was crazy. This put pressure on me. During that week, I was strong and did not see him, but when the weekend arrived, I craved to see him. I was disappointed as he never seemed to be around. Did he go back to his parents' place? Most German students did not go home on weekends. In order to relax I went away with friends for the weekend. This helped. I made sure I saw friends so as not to think of him.

One day, Stephen suddenly appeared at my door. I invited him in. Once in and chatting, he commented, "You are not in much at night".

"What do you mean... how do you know?".

"Well, I didn't see the light on in your room".

I liked this, as it meant that he was paying attention to me.

He said he came to see if he could help me with my German. Perhaps we could do an exercise on listening and writing.

Anything to keep him there. I giggled and said, "Yes please".

Stephan read a paragraph from an article, I wrote it down, and he corrected my grammar. We were studious for a while, until we kissed. Two hours later we stopped. I was drunk for him. I did not know how Stephan felt because he was quite casual. After that, we went for a walk. Being early spring the breeze was cool, but my heated heart kept me warm.

Previously, I had only had one love experience. Although it ended badly, for a time we were devoted to each other. After I arrived in Germany, I met Matiyas, whom I liked, but there was something about him that I did not trust. And then there was this man.

Stephan placed an arm around my waist. I had to stop myself from turning and giving him a full hug. Although my intuition told me that Stephan was not trustworthy, yet, I was still tender towards him.

Upon returning to my dorm door, I could still feel the flush of my face. His face was relaxed, his eyes filled with smiles. He was still gently holding my waist – one of his hands touched my face, the other hand turned me towards him. His hand caressed my neck, my whole body became soft.

Stephan was trying to make me horny. I pushed him away with all my strength. When he saw the disappointment on my face, he touched my face, "Mei, I am casual to other women, but to you I am serious." I screamed in my heart with pain, "How can you be casual with other women, but still want me", but I could not say it, and asked if he will come to see me again. He said he can only see me next Tuesday. Although I would have to wait for a week, I nodded my head and agreed.

On that night, I waited with a rose. When he did not come I went outside to see if his light was on. It was dark. I had a nervous stomach while I was waiting. At 3.00 am I went to knock on his door. When I raised my hand, I saw his key in the door. I opened and entered and found him on his bed.

Surprised, he asked, "Mei, is that you?"

I sat on the side of his bed, and could see him in the moon light. "Where were you, we had a date?" I wasn't angry, just disappointed.

"Oh yes, sorry, I forgot, I went to a friend's party".

How could he forget our date? I got angry. But still, I asked him if I could lay down beside him. Stephan lifted up the quilt to accommodate me. "Mei, you're trembling, your body's hot. Are you okay?"

I answered, "I waited outside for you for a long time, now I have a pain in the stomach". He did not seem to care too much and started to caress me. It seemed that he was familiar with a woman's body. I said nothing, I felt a little better from the stomachache. Under the moonlight, Stephan was quiet.

From then onwards I gave up the hope of love, but I indulged my affection. I told myself "It's all right, let the future be what it would be. No need to talk about the responsibility of belong to each other. Let myself enjoy his gentle touch", and indulged in the sex.

Over the weeks I relaxed a bit and was not as shy. I did want to see him, but most weekends he seemed not to be around. This depressed me and I could not understand why he would not see me. Occasionally, he was cold to me, which made me sad. But I didn't know what to do. Did he just use me for one night? I really felt that he liked me, and he knew that I was attracted to him. But I was burning up inside with worry.

Soon I got the answer. I found out that Stephan went home most weekends to his parents. This worried me more as I wondered if he had a girlfriend at home. If not, why would not he stay and see me? I didn't say anything – I couldn't. I just told him that I wanted to be with him all the time. I asked him how he felt. Stephan looked at me, his eyes soft, when he said that when he is with me he only thinks of me. But he was looking at me as if he wanted to say something more, but said nothing.

The next time we were together, Stephan opened up and told me he had a girlfriend. They had been together for a few years, that's why he went home every weekend. He went on to say that he did not care about this girl very much. I had already decided that I would not take Stephan serious anymore. Yet, it was Stephan who was the one who clung to me.

We went to see the French movie, *The Lover*, which was from the autobiographical novel by Marguerite Duras. Sitting beside Stephan as I did, it was the first time in my life that I understood the concept of

"Valentine"; I experienced the pain, the pain of not being able to have him in reality. It was really painful.

For a period after that, no matter what we were doing, having a walk or cooking together, we both almost simultaneously sung the theme music of *The Lover*, and enjoyed the memory of the movie. Sometimes, the air around us became frozen, we watched each other, I could feel that my body was burning inside, but I always held my lips and told myself "You are a Chinese girl, you would rather burn yourself into ash, but not allow yourself to became a pile of soft mud, without backbone".

I decided to leave. To move to another city. When I told Stephan that I am going, our conversation became cold and tense. In the end, Stephan said, "Mei, I will drive you to your new university. I will stay for a few days and only belong to you". I refused, I decided to start my new life on my own.

He gave me the piano music he composed as gift. I took it and put it at the bottom of my case. Since then, I have never opened it.

I told a Chinese friend of mine of these men, Stephan and Matiyas. After my telling, it seemed that those two stories were now past clouds, dissipated. I mumbled to myself, "I don't listen to Stephan's piano music. Matiyas said he would play the piano for me every day. I really want to listen to piano music for my entire life, but I listened to none". Then my friend asked me, "Do you really need to love a man who plays the piano?"

JIM

It was later when Jim came into my life. He played the piano, and really brought it into my life for the first time. While Jim first was attentive, it was his academic brain that attracted me to him. He majored in Engineering. In his bag there are always books, and if he did not have a bag with him, there would be a book in his pocket (in Germany, there is a small book, which fits in the pocket, called a tiny book).

His books were on all sorts of topics. I did not read many as I preferred classics. From his early childhood, his parents subscribed to the well known German weekly magazine *The Mirror*. Jim's reading list was influenced by the magazine's recommended bestselling books. The only exceptions were books by Zweig and Hemingway. Those were his favourites.

Jim only read books in the original language. He spoke German, English, French and Spanish. For a time I studied engineering at University as well, but I did not spend as much time studying physics, as I spent most of my time in the library reading the classics. I wanted to discuss these books with Jim but he seemed not overly interested.

In British literature, the Bronte sisters› books were my favourite. The first book I read was *Jane Eyre*. I told Jim, when I attended the Chinese university for my bachelor and post graduate degree, a lot of university girls loved the passage from *Jane Eyre*. I read it to Jim, '*Do you think I am a machine? A machine without feelings? My soul is the same as yours, my heart is the same as yours? I am standing in front of you and talk to you.*

I am talking to you, not through customs, routine, not even through a normal person's body. I am talking to your spirit through my spirit. It likes that we both pass a tomb, we stand in front of God, we are equal – because we are the equal'.

After reading it with the enthusiasm that I felt for it, I looked up at him and asked, "Do you understand, we are equal?", but I could see the confusion in his eyes. He said, "I have read Jane Eyre, but never took her with any seriousness. Your reading aloud is very good... Why do you like this paragraph? Aren't you equal with your Chinese boyfriends?".

I was choked by his question. I could only say again that this was writing from the heart. "Don't you pursue from the heart?", Jim ignored that and went on to tell me that *Robinson Crusoe*, written by Daniel Defoe, was his favourite novel. He suggested that I get a copy and read it. I thought, life is hard at the moment, and I have no time to read such a big book for enjoyment.

We talked about French literature, such as the classic novels of Hugo, Balzac, Dumas, Stendhal, and Merime. I told Jim that in high school, one of my set books was the novel *The Necklace* written by Maupassant. In this, the poor public servant's wife, Mathil, borrowed a diamond necklace from her girlfriend. She wore it to a ball of the elite. Unfortunately, she lost it. She had to borrow money to buy a real diamond necklace, which cost a fortune, so she could return it to her girlfriend. She was reduced to becoming a servant, washing clothes for over ten years to make up the money to pay the loans. She became an old woman before her time, with very rough hands. There was one day when she met her girlfriend on the street again. Her girlfriend told her that the diamond necklace was a fake and only worth of 500 franc. When I arrived in Germany, I saw many jewellery stores. All the pieces looked brilliant, but without a professional eye, it was hard to tell if they were real or fake.

Jim did not show much interest in the books I had read in my youth. He said, but with respect, "Aha, you read novels like these in your school years". I was so disappointed and replied, "How come you didn't have these books at school? After all, they are classics... It is sad that our reading interests are so different, do we have no common interests?"

In order to have common interests with Jim, casually, I introduced the novel *Lady Chatterley's Lover*. I secretly read this novel when I was in my postgraduate years. Many male students were attracted to this book, and I wondered if it interested him. It seemed that he was not overly interested. He did not realise that I wanted to discuss the author's intimate passages. Jim only chuckled and said, "Aha... I have read the book. I have also read D. H Laurence's *Sons and Lover's*."

I felt a bit embarrassed and upset about his, "Aha". What does he mean 'Aha'? We both love reading but have no connection with what we read.

One of the few Chinese sentences Jim learnt was, "Would you like some flowers?" When we wandered the streets after a movie, he would ask me in poor Chinese, "Would you like some flowers?" I would reply "Yes please", and he would buy a bunch for me. This made me happy. In the beginning, he bought whatever flowers were on offer. But as time went by, the flowers he bought became more specific. Jim told me proudly that he' was not satisfied with the normal flowers from florists. He needed to choose flowers and make special bunches for me.

I praised him by saying, "Since you started to buy flowers for me, your appreciation of flowers has improved. The same with clothes. Look at the way you now dress, much more stylish… even handsome". He looked a bit embarrassed but mumbled happily, "What, what did you say… really handsome? Hey hey, I am even more handsome when naked." I hit Jim's chest with embarrassment, but more and more frequently, Jim gave me his flowers. He brought me flowers to the hospital.

Although our literary tastes were different, we would talk about books. On the weekend we rode our bikes, and in the evenings went to concerts. After the concert he would give me flowers. But what attracted me the most were the times when Jim played piano for me.

The first time Jim came to visit me, he sat at my landlord's piano and started to play. The music melted me and I could not help but dance. There were the three of us, my landlord, listening, Jim playing, and me dancing. That was a lovely afternoon, with sunlight streaming in from the large window, warming the décor and our hearts as this young German man played.

It seemed that music was in his blood. He loved the piano and played as often as he could. Soon after I met him, one night in a pub, Jim went straight to the piano, sat down and played – when I saw his long gentle fingers under the soft light, that was when I decided to marry him. What made Jim love me as much as he did? I never asked him this question.

To Jim, running 42km marathon, riding his bicycle, skiing, surfing, diving, reading and music are tools for life. Not to show off.
He loved riding his bicycle through many beautiful and remote, cross country and road, cities, villages and rural. He always carried a few books, some biscuits, chocolates, and a big bottle of water in his bag.

In the Chinese community of Germany, there was a scandal. A Chinese female student took up with a German man. It was said that the man was not an old man, neither an ugly man. In fact, he was tall and handsome. He does covet Chinese girls though. Adding to the scandal was that the man's family were wealthy. They lived on the bank of Elbe River, in the expensive Branconi area of Hamburg. Previously, this girl studied under a well known Chinese Master in China. Being determined to continue her studies she came to Germany to study for her doctorate. It seemed though, that she could also study in bed, or so the rumours said. This German man is love-struck, and after just one night wants to marry her. The rumour spread far and wide, and it seemed that the entire world knew. At first, it was only Jim and I, who did not know. The female role in this rumour was… me!

Actually, the first time we made love, we almost broke up. When I was almost out of my mind with desire, Jim, always rational, with precision, took a condom out of his wallet. My eyes nearly popped out of their sockets. I asked him, "Goodness, how many ladies have you slept with?"

Jim laughed and replied "About twenty".

"What…Go, get out".

Jim realised there was a problem, but still laughing, "Then fifteen".

"Go, sleep under the bed".

Jim laughed louder, "What about ten".

I was upset, and for a time would not let him touch me. In my mind, I was scared that I would not compare to any of his twenty past girlfriends.

The next morning, Jim opened his eyes and said, "This is nice, very nice… Do all Chinese girls have magic?" I sighed in my heart, "I had one boyfriend in my study years in China, and we were not really sexually active, so my sexual experience was zero. Not like you, having dozens of girls".

After arriving in Germany, I went to the library and looked at a sex technique book. China did not openly have these. I was so curious and sat in a corner of the library and without realising it, spent hours pouring over these books. In reality, I couldn't automatically combine the Chinese and German way together. I treated making love like a serious performance, where the bed was the stage. Once on the bed, you started the overture, then Allegro, slowly, interlude, climax, and the finale, where the action should follow the heart. I felt that making love should not be like an experiment in a chemist's laboratory. When you get into the laboratory, if you want to change a colour, you take up the bottle and drop another chemical into it. When starting, the overture, you can still be so relaxed to find a condom in your wallet; I could not understand this at all.

In order to educate me, Jim took me to have a drink with his friend Wolfgang. When Jim asked Wolfgang how many girls had he had slept with, Wolfgang laughed in surprise, but with glee said, "About thirty. I started when I was seventeen". Jim looked at me, and fluttered his eyes, pretended to be neglected, "Life is unfair. Some die through over eating, some die through starvation. Wolfgang is always full, but me, poor me, I'm always hungry!"

I asked Jim if he had ever made a girl pregnant. Confidently, he said, "Never, I always have condoms with me, as you saw. When I was sixteen my mother had a chat with me. Amongst other things, she hammered into me always to use a condom. But to be honest, I was slow, compared to Wolfgang, as I was nineteen when I started".

Jim and Wolfgang drank their beer and laughed loudly. They loved this conversation. I was upset and wanted to take a beer bottle and hit both on their heads.

Jim told his parents that he had a girlfriend, and that she is Chinese. His parents were curious, especially his mother. She asked Jim to bring me to her home some time so we can meet. I was scared. I was Chinese, they were German, I did not know what to expect. I made all kinds of excuses to avoid going. But one Friday Jim called to chat. When I asked him how we were to spend the weekend, he declared, "Well, tomorrow, which is Saturday, my parents are coming to Frankfurt… Their main purpose for coming is to meet my Chinese girlfriend!" It sounded to me that Jim was also nervous.

The next day Jim's parents arrived. His younger brother, who was also a university student came as well. Normally, young German students arrange their own weekend, seldom being with the parents. It seems that Jim's younger brother was just as curious to see what his brother's Chinese girlfriend was about.

To me, Jim's parents looked like movie stars, as they are tall, slim, and graceful. Jim's surname is Goodhouse. I addressed Jim's father as Mr. Goodhouse out of respect. He was very funny, but clever when he said, "Forget how much money there could be in a 'good house' but rather look at the wisdom that makes a 'good house'.

Jim often told me how much he adored his father. He studied the same major as his father did. With obvious pride, he said his dad was a world renowned professor in his field.

Jim's mother seemed open-minded. She had given birth to four children, yet her body was young for her age.

The five of us visited the *Frankfurt Contemporary Museum*. It was built in 1981. The first principal was Jean Christophe Ammann, who was famous art historian. Ammann was an assistant to Harold Szeemann, who was also recognised as a great artist and dynamic curator. Ammann later became the principal of *Lucent City Art Museum* of Switzerland. Under his guidance, the fame of the museum grew.

When I observed the work of Joseph Beuys, who was a highly valued contemporary artist world wide, I explained, "Every five years, the art show of Cassell Literature and St. Cathedral Art – St Paul's Contemporary in Venice, are biannual shows that are considered to be amongst the finest contemporary exhibitions worldwide. Beuys' first exhibited in the Cassell Literature gallery in 1964. In later years, some of his exhibits were non-moveable art works. On his fifth art show, he became known as the monkey king and stirred up the show. He, sitting in front of his work, called *Organizing the Vote of Citizen for Direct Democrat Information Office is*, where he dialogued and argued with the audience daily for 100 days. On his sixth Cassell Literature Art Show, the work, *Honey Water Pump at Work Site* attracted the largest audience. Beuy's dug a hole several metre's deep and installed two water pumps in the hole. The one pumped honey, via a pipe to the roof, whereas the entire exhibition centre was covered in sweet honey. People questioned, is this art? On the seventh art show, Beuy's felt the exhibition space was not big enough. He said he needed more space and declared that his work would not be in the museum. Instead, he moved it outside. He utilised 7000 oak trees. But first, he brought in 7000 rocks and piled them in a corner of the area. At the commencement of the art show, Beuys planted the first oak tree himself. He placed a stone in front of every tree. His great environment protection artwork attracted artists and normal people. The finished product antagonised many, some activists dyed some stones pink, and threw some in the river.

Beuys passed away in 1986. In 1987, on the 8th Kassel Literature Show, his son planted the last oak tree beside the first tree his father planted. It took five years for the completion of the exhibit, when the 7000th oak trees were planted. On that same day, there was another Beuys' art collection held at the *Frankfurt Contemporary Art Museum*, which was *Stir up Heaven*. In China, we called him Wukong Sun (Monkey King), where he took all the monkeys from the 'fruit flower mountain, playing wildly all over the mountain. This is the exhibition that is now in front of you."

Jim's family were entranced by my explanation. His father's eyes gleamed. He praised me when he said, "Mei, it's really interesting to listen to you, a Chinese girl, explaining about German artists".

The next day, Jim told me, "My parents like you… they think you are so smart. And, I can tell you that intelligence is one of the main character traits that they are looking for in their daughter-in-law. They liked you, especially Mum".

I was confused, as I hardly spoke to her. I mostly talked with his father. I wondered if it was because of the joke I told Jim's mother regarding a Chinese friend. This friend is over sixty years old. She is a theatre dancer, and always dresses in the latest fashion. She is slim, but her face is covered in wrinkles. From behind, she looks like a teenage girl. Anyway, on the bus one day, a young man, who was behind her, flirted with her. When she turned around, and took off her sunglass, she said to the young man, "If you opened your eyes, you can see that I am a grandmother!" The young man was horrified. Because Jim's mother was not that old, I only told her the first part of the story, ignoring the latter part. I praised that her body shape is like my dancer friend; that she looked like a teenager girl.

Since that day, our relationship deepened. As Jim's parents came all the way to visit me, it would be impolite if I did not go to visit them. I also was looking forward to getting to know them all better.

We Chinese always offer presents when we see friends. Because I knew that Jim's entire family play and sing music, on that first visit the gift I took was not music, but a Chinese gourmet meal, which they were delighted with. At that stage, I had a Chinese friend who had recently opened a Chinese restaurant in a suburb of Frankfurt. He always asked me to help him study German. I did, and never for payment. This time though, I asked him if he could give me a Peking duck as a gift to take to Jim's family. My friend laughed loud, "Of course. You helped my German so much that it would be right if you asked for ten Peking ducks. Just tell me when you need it and I will make the best meal for you. I will get it ready for you to pick it up on the day". Which I did, and it was a beautiful meal. They all enjoyed the duck and kept saying how delicious it was. They were grateful for my gift.

Again, Jim told me that his parents gave me a very high score. "Ha ha", I laughed, "I was always good at tests since I was a kid". Jim treated me even better. I never expected he would care so much about his parents' opinion of his girlfriend.

After we married, Jim told me, "My parents wanted to know how smart you were, your wisdom, and if you were polite and respectful. Previously, my parents were never against my girlfriends but they were never particularly good to them. Now, they like you more than they like me!" He must have really felt this as I could tell there was a bit of rancour in his words.

Jim wanted me in his life, but did not want to commit, so he did not propose to me straight away, but he had his way to hold onto me. He gave up his comfortable single apartment and found an apartment for us to live in together.

In this de facto relationship, I felt that I had a home with another person for the first time. But it was disconcerting because apart from a piano he purchased – for which he sent the bill to his mother- he had no interest in us decorating together. He said, "Mei, you can decorate anyway you want, but it must be environmentally friendly". This was the first time that I was to decorate a home.

After I graduated from my Master's degree in China, I earned 10,000 RMB that first year. That amount was around ten times more than an average worker's wages. I planned to save my money. But when I was to go to Germany to study, I used the money to buy my plane ticket. I changed the rest of what I had into US dollars and took them with me. When I arrived in Germany, I spent my own money setting myself up. I earned little money from my casual job. Spending Jim's money to decorate made me feel uncomfortable. So I wanted to spend less money than it should have been. I also needed to achieve Jim's desire of environmentally friendly, which always costs more. I panicked a bit.

Soon though, I had made my plans – all the furniture was to be simple; and the appliances had to be economical. I made use of an old wooden study table of Jim's. This was going to be our dining table. It was the right size and had triangular wooden supports to support it. Although simple, I felt that it would be practical and looked fine.

To maintain the wooden theme, and whilst saving money, I asked Jim where I could order a wooden board and have triangular wooden legs cut. He told me to go to Bauhaus, a shop in Frankfurt.

At first, I was confused because I only knew of the German academic art school with the same name. How could they supply me with wood, and in the form that I wanted it? But then he explained that there is another Bauhaus in Frankfurt, which is a shop selling timber.

Bauhaus was in the city centre, some distance away. I needed to take the bus. It turned out that they were also a hardware store, with all sorts of tools. There were so many varieties of tools and equipment that I had never seen in China. I ordered all the wooden boards and pieces, cut to my measurements. A week later, I had to take the bus twice so I could get it all home. When all was assembled, it was perfect.

I cooked dinner for Jim every day and enjoyed it on our dining table. I always planned our dinner for 7.00 pm. Normally Jim arrived home at 6.30 pm. If he was late, even if only five minutes, I would complain. I would use my spoon and tap his head when we were eating. "I put all my heart into cooking a nice meal for you. No less than what you put into your work… You should arrive home on time to appreciate it." Jim would mutter, "Yes, yes, the meals you cook are all delicious."

One day I cooked stewed pork with orange and capsicum. I used the juice and skins from 2kg of oranges. I thought the green and yellow colour, with its sour taste, should fit the German liking for sour food. However, when Jim tasted it, he threw it in the bin. When I saw the horror on his face, I laughed so much it hurt my stomach. I teased him, "When I was a kid, in order to cure a cold, my mum cooked steamed pork with the whole orange including the skin. I remembered it was so delicious. This morning I noticed you had a sniffle… I cooked this specially for you".

I went to the Bauhaus shop a few more times. I was learning what they could offer. I ordered a customised bookshelf and other things.

Then I learnt that this Bauhaus Shop is in fact an extension of the Bauhaus Art School. It transpired that this shop is all over Germany and is famous worldwide for its architectural arm. One of the things I liked doing in the shop was to browse their tools. These were amazing.

I heard stories that if a girl was to decide on a good German husband, normally they would check if he is a good handyman! In the basement of almost every German home, there is a full array of tools. Some people even build a tool shed in their backyard, just for storing tools. We could never do that in China.

There was one time I went to the home of German friends. I asked them what they planned to do on their holidays. The husband showed me a corner of their living room; it was stacked with tiles, plaster, and tools. He told me, "We're not going anywhere this year. We only have a small bathroom next to the living room. I will expand it. I will add a shower. I only can do a little bit after work at the moment but I have five weeks› holiday due to me and I will use my holiday to complete this". At that time, I had not been in Germany for long and was surprised that this man could do all these things. Jim was an exception. Apart from pumping up the tyres on our bicycles, he did not like to repair anything around the home. He said he had too many hobbies, such as running, mountain climbing, skiing, surfing, diving and more.

Jim praised my diligent and creative decorating job. I told him that with Bauhaus it was easy. I never imagined the praise he gave me when he phoned his parents, "Mei furnished our apartment for almost nothing…" he over exaggerated. Two years later, in 1995, we moved to Berlin, where again, I furnished through Bauhaus, all very cheaply.

Even so, it was still many German marks. It has been over a decade now, and still the surface of the table is smooth and new looking. The previous Bauhaus table was moved to the storeroom downstairs. I literally furnished the house from the local Bauhaus shop, which was probably a third of the costs elsewhere, with our fridge, washing machine, and many other items. I felt it important that we had a nice modern looking house, and at a reasonable price.

After a while, Jim's parents asked if they could visit our Bauhaus furnished home in Frankfurt. Because we had nice décor, I wanted to serve a good meal for our guests.

I planned and worked hard for a successful meal.

When they arrived, I served them apple pie, which I cooked. Apple pie is popular in Germany. Because I had Jim, and his family, I wanted to learn German cooking and so started with the pie. I mixed the flour with water, butter, eggs, and sugar according to the recipe. Stirring all with the mixer. Then at the right time I put the dough in the oven, baked for the required twenty minutes. Once ready, I had the base. All it needed was the apples, cut before, place inside, put in the oven for fifteen minutes, and perfect. Simple freshly baked apple pie. They enjoyed it.

Then for the meal, I cooked a soup and the main course; it is called 'three meat fried'. This dish consisted of pork, beef and chicken, red, yellow and green capsicum, diced, and all fried together. I had chopped these up before they came. The sauce was made with ginger, garlic and spring onion. The source was added specifically for them as the authentic Chinese dish does not have the sauce. I added it because German people like dishes with a sauce. I served it up with white rice.

With the colours of the three capsicum types, all with the steam rising, it looked brilliant. Jim's parents really enjoyed it. The desert was ice cream, mixed with Chinese sticky rice balls. Everyone had three spoons of pink strawberry, green pistachio and yellow butter ice cream, with two round white sticky rice balls.

When I arrived in Germany, my cooking style was a mix of Asian and Western. I always used my own intuition, and it usually came out as I hoped. When the time came for them to say goodbye, Jim's mother told Jim, "Jim, since you left home, you have never had such a tidy home … nor such good food, you have never had it as good as this. It's all Mei's efforts. You should treat her well."

They also appreciated the house decoration as well, saying it was even better than what Jim had told them. Jim's eyes sparkled with pride and happiness. He spoke proudly, "Mum, when you and Dad visit, Mei tries her best to treat you well. Look at how well equipped our kitchen is… as good as yours". His mother laughed, "Good, good, if you need anything else, go with Mei to buy things from Bauhaus, anything you need in the kitchen… buy it. Then send the bill to me".

I felt that since Jim had fallen in love with me, Jim's mother treated him better than before. She was satisfied and most generous. In China, after I got my first wage, I gave it all to my parents, and even bought them a colour TV. I was not used to ask for things from my parents, like the German young people do. I admired Jim's parents who were educated and wealthy. My parents were normal working class people in China. Because of this, I was frugal, even with small things. A few years later, I remembered that the dish I used to cook that meal with was looking worn. I regretted that it was not the best quality. For example, I was stingy, never buying the best meat. I never bought king prawns. But I really wanted to cook the best meals for Jim's parents and so I spent a lot of money on that meal.

Jim supported environment protection, so much so, that he never bought a car. He rode a bicycle, an expensive bike. In 1992, after he started to work, his first purchase was a bicycle with all twelve gears. And then, once I became his girlfriend, he gave me a bicycle.

Although the price of this bicycle was not as expensive as his, it was considerably better than the one I had. He wanted me to be able to keep up with him, and to look good. Often, on weekends, we rode around the city, or out to the rural areas. It was such fun. If our destination was a bit further, we took a train with our bikes. Once we arrived at our destination, we disembarked and rode to the local sites. We rode through the small villages and the forests. The areas we rode were hilly but not mountainous. The longest and furthest we rode was along the Romantic Road in Germany. Every day for a week we rode an average of six hours a day, covering 120km a day. These had large hills, where the downhills had to be ridden with caution, after a grinding uphill ride. In the afternoon we pulled into roadside motels and stayed the night. One day, there was a violent storm. Even though we had wet-weather gear, we still got soaked, as we needed to keep on schedule. It was really difficult and painful with the rain splattering my face. There may have been a few tears in there as some felt salty and bitter. It was hard work and my muscles were screaming for a rest. Jim sometimes took the lead, but he always pushed me.

Afterwards, when we finally found a village to stay, I showered, and hung my wet clothes in front of the fire to dry for the next day's grind. Then I complained, "It's too long; I get bored, my bottom is raw, all my muscles hurt, I could sleep for a week". Jim teased me, "Maybe I should get a German girl. She won't complain. You are useless".

We traveled to cycling destinations by train, with a backpack. Jim would hang his bicycle (and mine) at the end of a train or put them inside the carriage. The longer cycle trips gave my bottom calluses!

GREEN WEDDING

Once I got to know Jim's family, I really liked them. However, my self-esteem was often low because of them. For our first Christmas together, I wanted to take Jim to China. Jim was as excited as I was. He was happy to escape from his parents for once. Before we went, Jim's mother sent us a white toy airplane with a nice card, "Dear Mei, Jim has always spent Christmas with us. But this year you are taking him to China. This pleases me. My present to you both is under the plane". I looked, and there was an envelope, tied to the plane with a silk ribbon. Inside, there was money for our plane ticket. This was unexpected. I looked at Jim. His eyes wide open in surprise, his eyebrows moving up and down. Later, he told me that his mother had never given him such a large amount like this.

On the 24th December, Christmas Eve, Jim and I boarded our flight for China. I held the toy plane, which I brought along. I did feel a bit sorry that we did not spend Christmas Eve with Jim's family, but I knew that Jim's younger brother would be there.

Christmas Eve is like the eve of our Chinese New Year. In the last few years I left my parents behind in loneliness. But my mother-in-law to-be had not blamed us for this, on the contrary, she gave us such a generous gift.

For all the latter festivals, birthdays, and things, I always received beautiful cards and presents from Jim's mother. I loved her more and more, perhaps more so than I loved my mother. As a child, when I had my birthday, my mother only cooked egg noodles, which were boring. She did sew clothes for me though, when we had Chinese New Years.

After I went to Beijing for university, I never received presents from my parents. Occasionally they wrote letters to me. But once I went to Germany, neither wrote to me anymore. I always had to call them on the phone. On those calls, I would say to them with sadness, and sometimes anger, "Why do you not write me? If I don't phone, I would hear nothing of your life. My mother in law loves me more, and is more of a mother".

After we returned to Germany from China, Jim's mother, holding my hands, asked in a half joking way, "Now that Jim has met your parents, how come he hasn't proposed to you? I thought Jim would give you an engagement ring in China". Jim's mother thought her son only went to China for that reason. Jim did not think so. He blamed his mother for the embarrassment she caused us both by saying that, "Mum, you care too much. Mei is still studying for her Ph.D. She has no job or income, I am not sure if I can afford to have a family at the moment". Jim was like many German men, they did not want to get married, they did not want to take responsibility.

Jim's mother laughed, and said to us, "Jim, you should be careful, a girl like Mei is not found very often. If you don't ask her to marry you, someone else will. You do not need to worry about finances, I have enough to help… I will support you". I heard her words, and she was right. Although I had never expressed this, I did have strong thoughts that if Jim did not take our relationship seriously, I would leave him. And, I probably would have done so without saying anything to him, as I was too shy.

What about Jim? After we moved together, Jim had paid for everything, rent, the decorating, and the piano. Jim had become addicted to buying flowers as well; he never asked me to buy flowers, he always bought them. Later, I even felt jealous of Jim's taste in flowers. I thought, because of me, Jim had become more refined, and gentle. He was more charming. Although I was feeling good about this there was always an underlying fear. I was fearful he would not ask me to marry him. Jim had too many advantages over me. He was born into a wealthy family. He had a good education and an excellent job – now, through me, he had learnt how to please women.

What about me? Having graduated from the best university in China, if I was in China, I would already be a professor and teach in a university. But I came to Germany to get my Ph.D. in art education. I loved this topic but I knew it would be hard to find a job after graduation, especially in Germany.

My family is not rich and cannot help me financially. The good thing though, is that Jim did not leave me in fear for too long. One evening he came home with a very special bunch of flowers. From his pocket, he extracted two engagement rings. They were inscribed, "Jim & Mei, 29th November, 1993". Then, he knelt on one leg, and dramatically said, in his rough voice, "3-3-3-4 (the beginning notes of Beethoven's Symphony No. 5, which many suggest is about fate – our fate)".

Stunned, I was silent until I asked him, "How come now?" His reply shocked me with its implication, "I'm afraid that you will run away from me… I have to engage you so you don't. But I don't know when I should marry you". I felt amazed at his foolish words and wanted to cry. The thought went through my mind, I knew Jim loved me, but why only have an engagement, and not marry? I would be well satisfied to marry him, in many ways I dreamed of a husband, to be a family member of this well-to-do and nice family. I liked Jim's parents, sisters, brothers. They were all talented musicians, they sang, all were with good culture. But I was too proud to ask Jim to marry me, to show him that I wanted to marry him. My self-esteem was too low. I did not say so directly, but I thought that if Jim did not treat me with his true heart, or wanted to marry me, I would leave.

I knew that Jim had many girlfriends before. They came from different countries. But Jim seldom took any home to his family. I was not as pretty as most of them. But I won him and his parents over, with my knowledge of many things, and more so, with my respect for them all. Jim's parents, loving their son as much as they did, saw that in me, that their son would get the best possible wife. They even treated me better than Jim. When Jim stood up to his mother and said, "You should not interfere in my business" and how he could not afford a family, Jim was not thinking about my feelings – I was never considered. The fact that his mother said not to worry about money pushed Jim to order the flowers and engagement rings. I was not expecting that things would happen so quickly. Yet, it was only for the purpose to keep hold of me. "Why is he so arrogant", I wondered. I felt sad, and forcefully took off the ring. Jim panicked, "Let's get married next year… next year we will get married".

I stayed, and half a year later we prepared to get married. It was faster than what I had expected.

There is one thing I must relate; the German custom of how new couples choose their own presents. This is very different from China. There are shops that provide such service from a present-list that the couple creates. The people in the shop would select all the items that are on the list and place them on a decorated table. All the invited guests go to the shop to choose the present they want to give. Then pay for the gift. For guests who lived in another city, there would be a gift list for them to choose what they would like to pay for.

At the time, I hesitated, but soon enough accepted the practical custom. We created our list and advised all our friends and loved ones which shop to go too. We asked for a twelve set of a well-known brand of tableware, including soup plates, dinner plates, and a matching salad bowl. But we did not specify all the rest. So after ten years of use, all the non-branded items, such as the coffee set, cutlery, etc. are not worthy any more for dinner guests. I have replaced all of these with better brands. These days the wedding gift table has moved from a shop to the internet. All guests need to do is login, check the gift pictures, and pull out their credit card.

We chose not to have a church wedding; ours was in the botanic gardens.

Jim's friend Wolfgang brought his cello. My friend Yezi, who worked in the Frankfurt Drama theatre, brought his violin. These two, who did not know each other, one Chinese, the other German, played in perfect harmony, Mendelssohn's *Wedding March*. In time with the melody, Jim and I, the new couple, led all guests towards the lake within the gardens. We entered a small boat and rowed the lake. There was a swing that we swung on. During the reception dinner, Jim's father, now my father-in-law, a famous professor, toasted us in accordance with German customs. Lastly, he said, "Let's raise our glasses... a toast, for our Goodhouse family now has a Chinese member... our daughter-in-law Mei...." He continued, "Now another toast, let us say cheers (prost) for Mei's parents, who unfortunately are not here today... we cheer them for producing such a good daughter".

It was beautiful, with the smell of the gardens, coffee, the food, the music, all surrounded by the greenery of those magnificent gardens. We were also surrounded with unlimited hope and endless dreams.

I was so happy that Jim played the piano. Not only Jim, Jim's father, his sisters and brothers all played the piano. I was willing to be Jim's wife, I was willing to become a member of this knowledgeable, artistic family. Jim loved me, Jim's family loved me. They gave me a new home, a new country, a big family. I appreciated that they all gave me so much warmth. I prepared to use all of my ability to support my tall Jim, to help him stand proud and love him forever. That felt really good.

On the day of our wedding, I wrote in my diary, "Jim is so pure and natural. I hope he will be happy forever to stay with me. I will be a good wife, and to be a good family member for the Goodhouse family".

I named our wedding" «The Green Wedding" in honour of Jim's love for the environment. After the wedding, all the guests, including his parents, brothers and sisters, left in cars. We rode home on our bikes!

A few years later when I reviewed my diary entry, I was shocked by my words – there was no happiness in them. I recorded my prayers for Jim, to be blessed – nothing else. Seems that the deep joy of marriage, only the day before, was forgotten, smothered.

To see if the couple can be a couple or not, the most important thing I think is how they continue, even if one has been difficult. And can they get along with each other without issues.

After work, the next day, Jim returned home, and before greeting me shouted, "Your bicycle is still downstairs. Bring it in, otherwise it will be stolen". I was concentrating on some writing I was doing, and mumbled, "« "Won't you bring it upstairs for me?" Again he shouted, 'It's your bicycle, you bring it upstairs". I frowned, "If you think that my bicycle has nothing to do with you, you do not need to remind me to bring it in… your reminder makes me unhappy". I smiled at him, and whined, "Pleeeease Jim, will you bring it up, I just want to finish what I am doing". Jim ignored me, and went to the fridge and grabbed a beer, as per his normal return-home routine. Plonking himself on the lounge he moaned, "I just bought up my bike… you must look after your own… you are selfish… lazy… wanting me to do everything for you".

Upset, and in a frustrated voice, I moaned, "How dare you say this, I do so much for you, and when I ask you to help me you call me selfish. You upset me. Forget about my bike, from now on I will leave it outside and let it get stolen. And when it does, I won't need to accompany you anymore".

Jim stood, and went outside. A few minutes later he pushed my bicycle in. I lifted my head, and looked at him, and laughed loudly. "Why are you laughing", he asked annoyed. I said, "I'll tell all females, that to see if their man loves them they must be unreasonable. Jim, you don't understand females. Because I was unreasonable, I will cook a lovely meal for you tonight".

My bicycle was not stolen. But after we were married, Jim wanted to stay home more. We rode less during weekends. Another hobby Jim enjoyed was mountain hiking and bush walking. There are many mountains around Frankfurt, and so we often went to one. All the these mountain trails are well marked, with a green circle to go around, or red triangles, sometimes, orange squares indicate the route.

The distances are also marked in kilometres. If your walking speed is 5km per hour, from A to B, and the distance is 15km, it will take around 3 hours. These signs always made me giggle. The mountain climber and bush walkers are all children of nature. The people who made those signs just want to make these children of nature happy, that's why they make so many colourful detailed signs – they achieved their aims. Jim could not understand why I found them so funny. But because I laughed, Jim was happy as well.

When we hiked, Jim always chose the longest route. I wanted to choose those which had a lot of café' on the route. Jim's persuasion to me was as if he was talking to a child, "Only 22km". I would encourage, "This track is only 20km, but there are 3 cafés on the way". We always ended up going his way.

I always became exhausted on his routes, tripping over my own feet. But when we did pass a café I was encouraged – the coffee aroma, pretty cakes with attractive names like Black Forest, fruit strawberry, chocolate cheese...... and most of the cafés had a great atmosphere, usually full of people on the weekend. The clientele were welcomed and always relaxed, all greeting each other as if old friends.

When we got back home, Jim always opened the piano and played. I generally went into the kitchen and prepared a nutritious meal to reward our exhausted bodies. The last song Jim played must be the famous German Song, Das Wandern ist des Müllers Lust. Encouraged by the enthusiasm of the mill workers, Jim said, "Mei, come over and sing… if you don't, I will sing with my hoarse voice". He knew that I teased him about his singing voice and that I would always drop what I was doing to sing.

**In Europe, I, the girl from Southern China learnt to ski. When Jim carried me on his back, skiing fast, I handed over my life to him.
Now, after the cancer operation, I go ski every year, where the exhilaration is mine alone.**

Often, sitting under the soft lights, Jim would leisurely browse the newspapers. One time I was feeling cheeky and said, "It must be so boring to have only one wife. Wouldn't you want a girlfriend as well?" He replied, "Women are troublesome. I had enough problems in the past. I'm so lucky to have you now. No, I don't need to have another, that's for sure".

But I am still interested, "You slept with many women before me. Do you miss them?" Jim was annoyed, "Don't ask these silly questions. I don't remember them anymore. If there is one woman I still remember, that is the one who I never slept with." Whilst saying this, there was an element of regret on his face. He then said to himself, "Enm, where are you now? What have you been doing all these years?"

Jim's answer made me jealous. I wanted to ask more about this girl, but he determinedly buried his head back in the newspaper in a way that said, "Shut up". A few minutes later, he took a swig of the beer I bought for him, as he pointed out the news of the day with loud laugh. My heart felt steady and the jealousies of his past lovers were erased. I was not worried about his past anymore. I was never worried when I was with him. In his eyes, I am pretty. I am pretty, even when I am sick. I am still pretty when I am cooking in the kitchen with hair falling into my eyes. I often joked with him, "There is a Chinese saying; the one that is in love, always feels that his lover is perfect. Even if I put a gunny bag on me, you will say I am pretty."

Jim thought my question about his past lovers was boring. He never asked me how many men I had slept with, or if I still thought of those men.

The reason I said that even if I put a gunny bag on me, and that Jim would still think I am pretty was not unreasonable. There is a story about this; I told earlier that when he started working he spent his first month's wages on his top model Dutch bicycle. One Sunday morning he took his petit Chinese girlfriend, me, not sitting behind him, but on the front bar, and embraced her as he rode. He was not likely to have been able to do this with a German girl, as they are too big. Jim was proud and felt smug when he put me on the front bar of his bike. He keep changing gears and accelerating to show off.

When I returned to China for a holiday, I saw most girls dressing in a feminine way. But I dressed simply. I spent most of my earnings from my part-time job on travel in Europe, and on concerts. On that day, I wore a coffee coloured woollen dress. I had bought the dress in China, and it had cost very little. It was a casual dress that covered my knee. I wore a thin belt of the same colour. The dress and belt gave me a nice shape, with prominent breasts, and a firm looking bum. I also wore a light blue silk scarf, which flew in the wind as we rode. When we passed the Bridge of Main River, we passed many people, all greeting us in a friendly way. It seemed to us that they said, "What a sweet couple". Right at that moment though, the scarf took flight and into river. He blamed himself for going too fast.

That scarf was used to add panache to my outfit. But Jim was so exhilarated, going faster and faster, whilst shouting in my ears, "You are so pretty... so pretty. All those people are staring at you... they can't take their eyes off you". I laughed happily, "If they are foolish, you are the same". There was nothing foolish about those people, they were just enjoying the spectacle of two people in love.

To me, love is everything. When I fall in love, I devote all myself to my lover and husband. But I realised that Jim was not the same. He treated me in accordance with how he was feeling at that time. After we got married, I wanted to continue working. I was anxious when I said, "If I can't find a job in a German company, I will work in a Chinese restaurant as a waitress". He said in a deliberate way, "Now that you are my wife, I don't want you to be a waitress." I was confused, why did he allow me to be a waitress when I was his girlfriend?

I knew a German couple, Sala and Teide (Teide was the man). They were both law students, he a few years ahead of her. They looked like models and complemented each other perfectly. Upon completing his studies, Teide opened a law firm, and did very well, whilst she continued her studies. As she did, she worked as a waitress, or sometimes she worked in Teide's law firm, and was paid very little. Occasionally, she modelled, all to get income from which to support herself. When Teide drank too much alcohol, he would complain that Sala spent too much of his money, and that it was his success that raised the quality of her life. Sala naturally was upset and moved out of Teide's luxury apartment. She rented a cheap unit, and continued her studies, and the part-time jobs as best as she could. Sometime later Teide went to find her, and they lived a de facto relationship for many years. When she graduated, she opened her own law firm, which was even more successful and profitable than his. It was then that Teide treated her better than before. They did not have children and their relationship was strong. I admired the fact that they got on so well after that rocky start and could put the past behind them without reservation. I liked this couple's determination – they fell in love, lived together, broke up, and then married. I was in admiration that Sala could forget how Teide treated her, and his insults. I liked her determination to complete her studies no matter how hard it was. They were a great couple together, with high incomes, and a luxurious life.

Jim was the same; a good husband, and later a good uncle to my boy, and after we married, our love was deeper.

FRUSTRATION, CULTURAL CLASH

Even though everything seemed perfect, we divorced. We were still young when we divorced. I suppose it is a waste of effort to keep thinking of this after the divorce. But I cannot help thinking about our time together. I have a compulsion to think about it. When I married Jim, I also married his family, a family I liked a lot. This family welcomed me into their bosom. By marrying Jim, I also married Germany, a country that I adored. I loved being a part of this life, country and family, it gave me an anchor, a feeling that I was not drifting anymore. A feeling of acceptance and acknowledgment. I had roots in the land, and I was happy.

This feeling made me want to be a good wife, a good daughter-in-law with a promising life. When I landed in this country, I started learning German from the basics. I wanted to learn diligently, to be successful. Although I had an almost perfect love and marriage life, it broke. The cultural chasms could not be crossed. I was under unrelenting pressure.

I related earlier that when I first fell in love with Jim, and when his parents visited, I worked hard to welcome them, and to give them nice presents, such as the roasted duck dinner. For this to happen, I had to take the metro, changing lines several times. This was a lot of money out of my precious income. To save money I did not pay the full fare. Unfortunately, the ticket inspector caught me. I lied to him by saying I brought the wrong tickets by mistake. I felt ashamed by my lying and regretted it. The inspector seeing that I was Chinese did not fine me as he should have done. The fine would have consumed several of my pay days. But I was kicked off the train.

Jim's family enjoyed the meal and complimented me for organising such a nice meal. I could not eat one bite, I was so ashamed. I came from a respected Chinese university, and here I was caught by a German inspector. How long does the feeling of shame last? To me, it will last my whole life. Even now, many years later, whenever I have Peking duck, or when riding the metro, the feeling of shame fills my gut. I knew what I did for my beloved people was good, yet I am not comforted by this thought. I try and reason with myself that at the time it was a nutty thing to do. But the problem is that I didn't grow up in the light happy drama atmosphere; most of my time I grew up reading of Shakespeare's tragedy and sublimity drama, and of feeling seriousness. I cannot completely overcome the feeling of shame.

I did my best to not fight with Jim. Most of the time I tried not to remember the triggers; if I do not remember the trigger, how could we fight? One time when we fought, he knew the right medicine to comfort me was by giving me a bunch of flowers. On this Sunday, after a fight, Jim hurried out. I was angry for him doing so as on Sundays the shops are closed. Where could Jim have gone? After a while, he rushed in and kneeled down, like he did when he proposed, on a single knee, and again, whistled the beginning of Beethoven Symphony No. 5 "3331…", then magically produced a bunch of flowers. His smile was broad as he told me that he had run to the train station, boarded a train to a station where he knew a florist was open on Sundays. A few happy tears wet my eyes, and I laughed with happiness.

Before we were married we hardly fought, but after the fighting grew over the weeks. One time he made the horrific statement that I only married him to get German citizenship.

This time, the tears were many, and their acid burnt my face. I hardened my heart and fought him, "If it's not for my Ph.D., I wouldn't have come to this country. If I didn't come I wouldn't know you. It was never my intention to stay in this country. Originally, I thought I would go to America after finishing my studies. All my university classmates have gone to America. Looking at it from a different perspective, I am smart and reasonable looking, why can't I stay in Germany? Why would Germany reject me, a Ph.D.? You, although you are a German, you are not the best at your work". I wanted to hurt him. Jim loved his job and worked hard. He always wanted to do well so he could receive acknowledgment and admiration from his family. What I said must have held some truth, as he started to cry. He was laying on the bed, face to the ceiling, staring and shouting, "Mei, you hurt me on purpose, you hurt me on purpose." When I, with my own tears running, saw Jim crying, facing towards the ceiling, I was shocked. This German could cry openly, facing up; we Chinese normally cry with hidden faces.

In China, I felt capable in my studies and to work. However, when I arrived in Germany I had no formal job. Whilst a student I did manage to work in a few casual positions, as a secretary or personal assistant in German companies. I was often praised by my work colleagues and bosses. They said I contributed many useful ideas. In the summer holiday of 1993, I went to work at Merck for ten weeks. Merck is a massive pharmaceutical company. At first, my wages were low, but I soon received a pay rise and staff benefits, such as annual leave and overtime. In that time I earned enough for an entire year's spending as a student. My boss, Dr. Dill, was a venerable man with a long list of important clients. He recorded every single client birthday. At Christmas, he offered no season's greetings, but he did give birthday greetings, and never missed one. Sitting together one day, we were chatting about these celebrations. I recited a saying that was believed to come from Confucius; *'When I am 10, I devoted myself to studies; when I am 30, I am independent; when I am 40, I have no doubts; when I am 50, I know my fate; when I am 60, I am easy going; When I am 70, I follow my heart but don't break laws'.* I suggested, "Why not offer those words to your clients on their birthday… They will appreciate the sentiment, irrespective of the age. Chinese sages recommend that we search our heart three times every day. In our busy lives, this heart-searching three times a day is likely to benefit ourselves."

Dr. Dill listened to what I said with attention and asked some questions. He did use the Confucius saying on that year's birthday cards, and sent them to over 200 important clients. He added a sentence, which said, "If you like this wisdom, it is my dear friend, Mei, you must thank".

Because of my Chinese upbringing, when I made a mistake, it was hard for me to acknowledge my error. When I performed well, it was also hard for me to ask for acknowledgment.

A few years later, I went to China for a family visit, where I received many job offers. Seeing other young Chinese people putting in applications, I was surprised at their lack of humility when promoting themselves. They wrote on their applications, and with full confidence, "Trust me, I am really capable; if you offer me the position, I will achieve the best for you". And, when these young people made mistakes, they were quick to say, "It's okay, it won't happen again". Then if they made more mistakes, they seemed relaxed.

There was a period when I felt that I was behind the times. It is necessary to express yourself in an appropriate language, but more important is to remain with both feet on the ground, whilst advocating yourself, whilst using the language of the advertisers.

I was good at my studies, from my childhood to university. Being settled with Jim, most days he spoke about what happened at work. A lot of time he laughed and also complained about his boss or colleagues. I could tell that there was something wrong with his communication skills. He was my husband, and I must be loyal to him, and encourage him. And, I cannot fully judge German companies, because I am not German. Nor do I want to attack my husband.

But now that Jim had hurt me by suggesting I was only with him so I could remain in the country, I fought back without sympathy. I told him that I felt his methods of communication at work were harsh. For instance, all the things that he said to me became a hidden sickness, which later resulted in our divorce.

Just before we were to get married, we went on a forest hike. The air was fresh, I was joyful and full of love, gratitude in my heart. "Jim", I said, "Your mother treats me so well, after we get married I want to call her mother as well". That's when he said, "How can you call her mother, she already has four children who call her mother"

I felt like I had been slapped and asked, "What should I call her then?"

"You use her name, that's what it is for". This was a natural answer for Jim.

"Carlin". I have to call my mother-in-law Carlin. Jim told me to do so. I felt helpless. On my first visit to Jim parent's home, in accordance to Chinese custom, I should call Jim's mother, Aunty. This is respectful. But it is different in Germany. Jim said in Germany it is appropriate to use her Christian name. When I did call her Carlin, it felt strange. In time, it became easier as I drifted into Western ways. But from the depth of my heart, I always felt a bit strange.

This raised another issue. I was worried he would call my parents by their Christian name – because Chinese custom dictates that Jim should call my parents, Mother and Father. I thought with concern, "They don't care of my intention to have them called Mum and Dad, so why should I insist he does as an insult to myself".

On our wedding day, Jim and I called my parents in China. I told Jim to call them Mum, and Dad. I never got over the awkwardness of calling my mother-in-law Carlin, as if I did not respect her.

On the day we married, I was so happy. All the guests were happy; the beauty of the gardens trees, and the friendly green environment. Green is the token of expectation and hope. But even with all this hope, I was feeling homesick. My parents did not come to my wedding. I did not plan to bring them across. It would have been too difficult, with visas and everything else, but more so, the cost. I was still a student and could not afford it. My mother-in-law told me, in Germany, it's the bride's side that organises, and pays for the wedding. "Mei, we love you as we love our daughter, we will pay for the wedding for you". In this situation, how could I put out that I wanted to invite my parents? I couldn't.

I was happy, but there was always pressure. Jim's father, who was my father-in-law, said, they give thanks to my parents who raised such a smart, respectful, and well educated daughter. He raised a toast to my parents, who live thousands of miles away. I myself should not have been concerned because of my parents not being there; after all, on my birthdays she only cooked me noodles, there were never prettily wrapped presents, they never bother to write me anymore. I missed my father's letters, his beautiful calligraphy, and news.

I needed his letters. He couldn't be bothered and was more willing to receive phone calls from me – it was easier. It was expensive for me, a student, to make phone calls from Germany to China. My parents did not want to call, and so they did not. All my relatives in China wanted me to call them, they are always excited and proud to receive phone calls from Germany. Living in Germany, as a Chinese girl, I was often lonely and wanted comfort from my parents and relatives. I was pleased to have been accepted by Jim's family. Of course, I could not share my disappointment with Jim or his parents. I could not 'lose face', I must retain my dignity. I could not ask Jim to treat my parents as well. I had to keep these thoughts to myself. I married Jim by myself, I married Germany, my parents did not come, and they would have been a burden if they did. However, every time, in the darkness of night, I felt loss and sadness. I could not erase those feelings, they were always with me.

If I had a child with Jim, I would have rooted myself in Germany. But when I mentioned a child, again he was brutal. Jim was 185cm tall, and handsome. I dreamed that our child would be tall and handsome. Jim raised an eyebrow, and half-jokingly said, "What, to give birth to a child with eyes as small as yours?". My dignity was shattered. I spoke to Carlin and told her what he said. She roused on Jim, "How foolish you are Jim. Yours and Mei's child will be beautiful. It will the best of both races". Jim, much chastened, with wide eyes said, "Mum, you are right... Mei is also good and healthy... she's good at all kinds of sports. Remember how quickly she learnt how to ski, she learnt faster than any German girl would".

When Tartan turned into three, Jim started to teach him how to play piano. At first, these were German songs for children, such as; *Swimming Little Duck* **and** *I Am Riding On The Horse Back"* **etc.**

I stared at Jim in amazement. In China, I was recognised as a beauty. I had the rare but coveted double eyelids, over deep eyes of wisdom.

How come Jim did not appreciate my eyes? When we first went skiing, his wife learnt so fast that the manager gave us the skis and entry for free. When we played group games, his wife's magical-skill amazed all his German male friends. She won all the games, and even made one German woman so jealous she went home. Jim was proud of me. So why would he not be proud of my face? Why did he say if we have a baby, it would have small, funny eyes?

I think Jim's big eyes are beautiful. But Jim thought my small eyes are funny, not good enough. From then on, I started to look at Jim's eyes in a more critical way. I started to feel that there was no brilliance in them, nor depth.

JIM'S PRECARIOUS JOB POSITION

Jim persisted with his belief that I only married him so I could remain in Germany. In return, I started to criticise him as not being very clever.

At the end of 1994, Germany experienced an economic downturn. The unemployment rate increased. Jim was to be transferred from the headquarters in Holzman. He had two choices; Leipzig in Eastern Germany, or the capital city, Berlin. I said to him that if he chose Berlin I would be okay, as I grew up in a capital city, Beijing.

In fact, I felt that Frankfurt, which is the financial centre of Germany, was too small. So we moved to Berlin, and into an apartment. Everything in Berlin was expensive, especially the rent. After the reunion of West and East Germany, the German people voted to make Berlin the capital city. The thinking of the time was that to create another capital city would cost a fortune.

To support our move to Berlin, Carlin banked 500 Marks into our bank account. We did not expect this.

The cultural life of Berlin was more to our liking. However, from a job aspect Jim was unsatisfied from the first day. There were more and more pressures on us. He had to get up at 6.00 am, to leave for work by 6.30, and only returned home around 8.00 or 9.00 pm. It was hard for us to have dinner and time together again. The wonderful days that we had spent in Frankfurt were gone. It was at this time when I completed my Ph.D. and started to write a monograph in Chinese. I dreamed of setting up an institute of cross-pollinating Chinese and German culture. Jim liked my cultural dream and appreciated that his wife stayed at home writing her paper. I also painted, which he liked.

He was proud of me, in front of his colleagues and friends, of me doing these things. However, with the economy being as bad as it was, Jim started to pressure me into giving up my art major, saying that it would be hard for me to find a job. He wanted me to switch careers to education, or to be a high-powered secretary. One of Jim's aunties worked as a CEO's assistant in Berlin in a big company. She was always dressed in powerful business suites and was very capable in that position. She earned a good income. Jim thought I would be good in this sort of job. When I did work part-time in some of those big German companies, my bosses always appreciated me.

Jim was always filling out bank deposit slips. On these, there was a question that asks, Who do you nominate as a beneficiary if you die? Jim always nominated me. When I saw these, I felt uncomfortable. He changed though, saying in a nervous way, "I have calculated my finances, and if I lose my job, I will travel around the world riding my bike. I only have enough money to support myself." My studies were nearly done with, and I suddenly felt that I had no future in Germany. Jim said to me without hesitation, "Forget about your University degrees, you are smart, you must be a secretary for a boss".

When I did get my Ph.D., it was with a high distinction. How could I just be a secretary?

I did not want to be a secretary.

The gap between us was widening. The economy was getting worse. Jim faced the economic situation with fear. Soon, the biggest building company, Holmanz, started reducing their staff. Hozmann, which had a 150 year history, with twenty thousand employees worldwide, was putting off staff. As an engineer, Jim was worried about keeping his job. We had not been in Berlin for a year when he applied for a transfer to a smaller company in the hope of escaping redundancy. Then, the German Chancellor, Herr Schroeder, allocated 2.2 billion Euro to try and save the company, but it did not turn out that way. Hozmann, along with other large companies, went bankrupt. Jim was transferred to another building company, and from being in an office, he was an onsite engineer.

This work site was restoring a historical building. It was on a famous street, where the Bodhi trees flourished at the Brandenburg Gate. When he started, I wanted to see it, and to support my husband I went to the site, and put on a hardhat. Jim gave me a tour of this national treasure of a building. The outside wall was cleaned and remained 'of the period'.

The inside was modernised. A few years later, every time I passed the building, with its historical facade, I felt proud for Jim. But the reality was also cruel – Jim was an office-nerd, and preferred the office, as opposed to the site. He did this for over three years. In those years, he lost onsite experience. It was not long until he clashed with his boss. But now, the competition was much fiercer and he was deeply concerned. In order to overcome this, he thought he would look for work in other parts of the world. The company did have sites in other countries. I was vehemently against this move, and argued, "Jim, we are like the opera drama, the *Drifting Dutchman*. Life is not an opera. I have studied all my life and want a rest from studying. If you go to another country, we will separate... If you go to Spain, or Italy, I would have to learn Spanish or Italian. I do not want to study any more. I want to settle down. I want to get a job, I want to have a baby. I want to have a stable home life. I do not want to drift anymore."

But Jim did not care about this, or bothered to discuss it with me, and applied for work in another city. After getting a position, he went, but returned every two or three weeks for a few days. He was like a big child. Whenever he returned, his travel bag was stuffed with dirty clothes. He would rather catch trains and airplanes with his dirty linen for me to do, than take them to a laundromat himself. And if it seemed that if I was not at the train station or airport to meet him, his face was long and irritated. But then he would see me holding a yellow rose waiting for him. Then, like a little boy, his face changed with relief, he would become so excited, he would hug me tightly and cover my face with countless kisses, one time making an earring fall off. Then we had to search the floor for it. The separation, though, was good in as much as we were always happy to be back together again. He would blabber, "Mei, Mei, I only want you. I want children with you, we will have a big family...".

A big family, two or three children – my dream.

But the reality was different. The weekends were always full of love after the lonely separation. Again though, it was not long before Jim had tension with his new boss. So whenever he returned, the happy time was unhappy with his emotions. We became strangers again.

At Christmas in 1996, and New Year of 1997, Jim decided to go diving for two weeks, without me! He felt that it would help him release his tension. I was annoyed as Christmas is a special time and we needed to share it together. I complained dramatically, "Don't you be another

Jose". I had told him the story of Sanmao and Jose (a classical Chinese story – Sanmao (Echo) was a Taiwanese author. Jose, her husband, died in a car accident) before. Jim just said, "Chinese girls are too sensitive." I did not want him go to diving, it seemed that I did not want him to be another Jose and die whilst diving. This would be the first time we did not holiday together. So, I went to America by myself – I spent US$1500 from our joint deposit account. Even though I had not worked since we married, it was considered ours. I did not feel guilty, as I had saved us a lot of money through my being thrifty. Jim knew that. But that was in better financial times. Because of the economy, Jim wanted a financial buffer in case he lost his job – he was angry. When I came back from America, I encountered his angry face, and a separation order. He told me I was not a good wife.

According to German law, to get a divorce, a one year separation must be had. He wanted to divorce me. I was terrified, but I did not beg. With dignity, I went to his lawyers and sadly signed the agreement. I only remembered what the purpose of the agreement was, and not one word of it.

Jim and I formally separated but lived under the same roof. We occupied separate rooms, but shared the living room and kitchen, like housemates. We got along with each other as best we could. Also, according to the German law, when separated, if the wife has no employment, the husband must give a percentage of his income to the wife to cover her living expenses. Jim acted in accordance to the law.

I marvelled that when we were boyfriend and girlfriend, I looked after the expenses with thrift, never spending anywhere near all of his salary. Every month for the entire time, we would deposit the excess into our joint account. Once separated though, we lived in the different rooms. I had plenty of money to spend, while not needing to do the housework if I did not want. That law did stop my self-discipline. Although separated, I still loved our home.

When I was born, my entire family lived in a small room of about ten square metres. There was a small shed outside, as well as the kitchen. I thought that unit was my parent's home when they married but it was not. In that place, there were two or three other people living there. My parents begged the other people to give them some space so they could get married, and so it was on their wedding night that they started to live there. When they gave birth to me, the company my parents worked for allocated them a unit of about sixteen square metres. The kitchen was also outside. This was common in China. Then when my sister arrived, we four lived in the unit together.

I do not recall ever being unhappy because of the small unit. By the time I went to high school, my parents company again allocated us another apartment, this time in a block of two units, one upstairs, and ours downstairs. It was around twenty square metres, with another thirty square metres of courtyard. My parents planted a tree at the corner of the yard.

A few years later, the shade of the tree covered the whole yard. My parents bred gold fish, cultivated a flower garden, and raised chickens. We two young girls had to feed the hundreds of fish after school. On the way home from school we went to a local pond to collect fat worms for the fish. The darker the mud, the smellier the pond. We had to dig into the dark mud, to extract the red worms. After school, we fed the worms to the fish, watered the flowers, and washed the chicken coop floor of muck. When the chickens gave eggs, they sang happily. Different chickens made different sounds, with either a short or long rhythm – a choir of chickens.

We had a table in the courtyard and ate many meals there. It was lovely with all the flowers and hundreds of fish leisurely moving through the water. We often ate fried eggs with home grown spring onions – delicious. But sometimes I was too motivated to improve my math to have or enjoy dinner.

Of course, at university, I was in a dormitory, sharing with six other girls. There were double bunks. There were occasional disagreements because of everyone's differing habits. Mostly though, we enjoyed our time together and became fairly close.

Then, at my postgraduate studies, I shared a room in a hostel with another girl. This arrangement was probably the best accommodation that any Chinese university offered at that stage. My roommate though, had a boyfriend, and so it was uncomfortable in that situation. I longed for my own private room.

Skating on Weiming (Unnamed) Lake of the Beijing University. As a girl growing up in southern China, we learnt to swim, catch worms, and be independent.

In Germany, the first dormitory I lived in was a single student room of about twelve square metres. It had a lounge that pulled out to become the bed. There was a shared bathroom and kitchen in the corridor. It was the first time in my life that I had my own space. Later, I tried to get a larger, fully apportioned apartment with an ensuite and kitchenette. The kitchen corner was tiny with a stove, refrigerator, sink and taps. That was the first time I felt totally independent in my space.

Then our apartment in Berlin was in a three-storied building; after World War II, Russia occupied East Berlin, and the Allied forces remained in the West. Our block was in the West, and it was said that an American lived in the apartment, as it was most comfortable. We lived on the second floor. It had not been painted for many years, and so I bought paint and brushes, covered my head with a scarf, climbed the ladder, and painted it myself. My mother-in-law's donation helped with the costs of renovating.

I purchased the sofa, carpet, dining table, bed, cabinets, etc., and in order to save the transport fees, I drove a big cargo van across the city to pick it all up. I assembled the furniture, and bought a big wide dining table. I used the table as my painting table. Finally, I hung beautiful paintings I painted on the wall. When finished, I cherished this home very much. After we separated, I still kept it tidy, even though the law dictates that I did not have to.

Jim found another girlfriend, and brought her to our home. I treated her with courtesy. But one time, Jim and his girlfriend finished a meal and left the dirty plates and mess. I got angry, then, probably in embarrassment, Jim also got angry. The girlfriend persuaded Jim to help clean up. By law, I am still Jim's wife, but being separated, we thought we were both free, and should not interfere in the other's private life. I was angry with him for bringing a girl into *our* home. Having this stranger in the apartment made me feel uncomfortable.

That women seemed to love Jim and this made me feel that I was not tolerant enough. I felt I had failed Jim. Since then, I decided I would try and not be angry with either of them. I did not always do this well, but I tried to not let it out.

A year passed, and Jim could now submit the divorce papers. But he did not want to be divorced. He wanted a reconciliation. The young girlfriend disappeared. Jim also said there was no long-term relationship with her, she hadn't even started university. He did not want another student wife. He was also aware that he could lose his employment, and what would he do with a young girl like that, she would be more of a dependence than he thought I was. So, we took up together again.

There was a Sunday, 16th August 1998 to be precise; we went to the new *Berlin National Art Museum* to see a Lyonel Feininger exhibition. Feininger, born in America but in 1871 came to Germany to study when he was nineteen. He remained in Germany, and Europe, only to return to America towards the end of his life. For the exhibition, there were 173 paintings. All were oils, landscapes of America, Germany, and Europe. Being such a full programme, many people were confused and did not know where to start. Because of this, Jim and I joined a guided group. After the tour, we wanted to sit and went to an outdoor café, where we chatted about the paintings, and the information that the guide gave us.

We both agreed that Feigerning's style was strange, especially the colour. All his paints were old fashioned – and the style was vague. Jim and I agreed that the tour guide was inadequate in his explanations, and that his knowledge was shallow. We felt dissatisfied because we could not understand Feigerning, or his reasons as to why he painted as he did.

Jim, trying to console me, changed the topic by raising his eyebrows in an engaging way, "Did you notice, among the audience, there was a very special woman?"

"No", I jokingly said, "I only looked at the men." Jim scrapped his chair as he bought it closer to mine, and lent in, putting one hand on my knee, whilst whispering, "That woman is not young anymore, but she's charming and stylish. Looks like she cut her hair herself, not so tidy, very short, all spiky, this gave her a unique look". I laughed, "You watched the charming old lady with more attention than you studied Feigerning's paintings?... Did you watch all the women in audience?"

Jim laughed happily, "Darling, no one can compete with you. They all listened to the guide's explanation and seemed just to want to fill in their Sunday. They didn't really enjoy it. Only you did". I enjoyed my husband teasing me about other women's appearances. He laughed again, "You are the only angel in the audience. You concentrated so hard... like listening to a passage in the Bible at church. I held no prejudice and reservations".

"It seems that you criticise our Chinese girls like rural girls?" I pretended to be angry, but was happy inside. I am surprised that despite Jim's calm demeanour, he was to the point.

We were getting on better, like our earlier times. I started to earn money, and our life was enjoyable. After we separated, I felt it important that to be independent I needed to get a job. For a time, I gave up my dream to create the cross-cultural institute I so desperately wanted. I spent a lot of time job hunting, and landed a job with a German training company. They provided training for high-end groups from Russia and China, where both countries were in transition periods. I did office management, translations, and other tasks.

Once the training for a group was completed, there was often one to two weeks touring for the group. I acted as their tour guide. When a member of the group made an expensive purchase, such as a watch or diamond, I received a good commission from the shop for taking the group there.

So, with my first job in Germany, I received a good income. I contributed to the household expenses, and was financially independent of Jim. I did not know if this was the reason why Jim started to treat me differently, and why he wanted a reconciliation. Just like before, on weekends, we went out to shows, theatres, hiking, and the other outings. This time though, when we ate out, I was not hesitant as I was before, worried that I was not contributing. We would go to restaurants, cafes, etc. but Jim felt no need for conversation. He would use a toothpick and bury his head in a newspaper or magazine.

THE NIGHT THAT CHANGED MY LIFE

How does a woman decide on a life changing event? This is forever a mystery. I have always had my direction firmly held in my mind. The same with morals and principals of life. In China, my life was calm and advanced without a problem – I mean real problems. I could have stayed in China and lectured in a University. But I had a dream to go abroad to study, and this dream was paramount. Or, it was the fashion at that stage to go to America or Europe. I got the chance to come to Germany, and did so without hesitation. When I arrived, I had no money and could not speak the language. Yet, I earned my Ph.D. in my thirties. I loved the arts, travel, and of course sport. I matched Jim in all these areas. However, after I gained my Ph.D. I suddenly got the urge to have a child. I was also pressured by what I thought was my advancing age.

Jim worked remotely for two years. Then there was that period when we were formally separated. After we got back together, I wanted to make our marriage solid – to have a child. But Jim felt that his job, and life, were not stable enough. He wanted to wait.

Wait? Women in their twenties can wait, but in their mid-thirties, they cannot! I could not wait.

There was another reason but it was difficult to tell Jim. Since being in Germany, I had moved more to that culture. And on occasions when I went back to China, I could see that it had changed a lot. Then, because I liked my job, I really wanted to make Germany my home.

I spent a lot of time trying to improve my speaking and reading of German. I forced myself only to read German books and work. Although I am still slow in reading German, sometimes too slow to trigger my interest, I continue with it. China was still deep in my heart. In the decade

I had been away, there were huge changes and I longed to participate in activities between China and Germany. To be an advocate for both.

When I did the cross-culture exchange activities, I encountered my Chinese love, Yun. It happened at the time when Jim and my marriage were shaky, when we had separated. It was at a time when I was most vulnerable.

I felt fear because of Jim's unstable job situation, and that his attitude would never allow him back into the relationship. I was fearful that I would miss my chance to have a child. The cultural belief of Chinese people is that not having a child was to be incomplete as a woman. I was starting to panic. We were taught that when a woman reaches my age, the body would be getting too old to have a child. I really longed to have a child. I wanted one with Jim. By doing so, we were committing to each other, and I to Germany. But actually, I should have been clearer and firmer with Jim.

In this frame of mind, I forgot the principals I had been raised to. I forgot them all. I was not thinking straight, such was my need to have a child.

On 25th September 1998, Friday, it was two days before the German election. The last campaign of The Social Democrat Party was held in Berlin. This was the night that changed my life.

For months I wondered; is this marriage the one I really want? Being with Jim was financially comfortable, even though I had to fight for my own financial independence. He cared little for my basic dignity. He wanted me to be a secretary. Did he feel threatened because of my education? He did not want my child because it would have funny eyes. Jim criticised China and everything about it. He maligned my people, all of which hurt me. When he came to China with me, he moaned constantly, like a child who was not allowed a sweet. He hated the large population, and thought that China was in chaos. In those days, in southern China, many of the buildings had no heating and he caught influenza. With his runny nose, he grimaced at the poverty of China.

I finally decided to divorce him. I wanted a baby, and one that was one hundred per cent Chinese. I would start again, to fight for my life, independently. I, and my Chinese lover, Yun, who later became the father of my son, were involved in the media for the electoral campaign. We two were the only Chinese at the event. Yun's major was broadcasting – he had a wonderful speaking voice. He worked part-time for the *Voice of Germany*, and *Voice of France*, as well as broadcasting to China.

It was my first time participating in such event, working for the media in the coverage of the election. There were TV and radio crews, as well as the newspaper media, all preparing to broadcast the event to the rest of the world. With photographers, and lighting experts, cables, and interviews; all amongst the milling public, who wanted to see what was going on. It was chaotic. The future Chancellor, Herr Schroeder, came on stage and made a speech. I was enthralled. Herr Schroeder's early life had been hard, and the way that he overcame this was, to my mind, the right credentials for a Chancellor. After he finished high school, he had to take a job as he could not afford university. But later he put himself through university. Then he became the Chancellor of Germany, mostly because of his fighting spirit. I did not go home that night. I decided that I would never live there from then on. The night before the German election in 1998.

With the intense emotion I was feeling, I found an excuse for my behaviour and decision. I felt that it was right to live with a Chinese man and have a child. This was my new start. I could either stay in Germany or go back to China, the choice was mine, I would be totally free.

Two days later, on 27th September in 1998, Schroeder became the 14th Chancellor of Germany by defeating Herr Kohl. Four years later, in the 15th Federal election of Germany, Schroeder faced many difficulties, and called an election. He was to face a very promising member of the CDU – the Christian-Demokratie Union, Herr Stoiber.

I had just returned from a trip to China, and after catching up on my post, saw the electoral notice. Still being jet-lagged, and having difficulty with the German instructions, I decided not to vote. On Sunday, I went to my friends, Lixin and Bain's home. It was Bain who came and picked me up. Whilst driving, Bain asked me if I had voted. After telling him no, he encouraged me to vote by using an electoral slogan, '*Your vote will decide who will be your next Chancellor of Germany*'. I looked at my watch, and said, "There is only ten minutes left till the closure of the election, there is no time". Bain, immediately spun the steering wheel, turning up a side road, and said, "Yes there is… there is a voting station at this primary school". At 5.58 pm, with two minutes to spare, I voted on my first German election. That night, at Lixin and Bain's home, we drank beer in front of the TV, whilst watching the counting as the votes came in. It was tense as it was neck and neck. Herr Stieber was just ahead most of the time. Yet, the TV broadcast showed both parties preparing for, either victory or defeat. We were on the edge of our seats, probably made more anxious by the beer we had consumed. Almost at the end of the counting, there was a dramatic turn-around, the Union Party of the Social Democrats and the Green Party. As a coalition, they gained the most votes. I voted for the coalition, and Bain shouted, "Mei, your vote decided the election!"

My vote may have made the difference, but who will decide my destiny? I wondered.

DIVORCED

Because of the unemployment pressure, Jim became too serious, all the time. He worried constantly about our finances, and that I was a burden, forever. When we separated, as mentioned above, Jim had asked me to sign a legal document saying I had no right to any of our assets, because without the agreement the courts decide who gets what property. I did not understand the logic of the law, but I had my own rules. To me, Jim asked for the separation, he asked me to sign the property agreement. These conditions pained my soul and shook the root of our marriage. I only dreamed of love, never of money. I knew that one day I would be a success through my own efforts, but at that time, I had not achieved that dream, and my marriage was broken. I was sad, and fearful.

Perhaps, this pressure, and the fear, resulted in the cancer a few years later. I was not aware of the pending cancer at that time. I held my breath, and gave up everything. I agreed, once I divorced Jim, I would not take anything with me, not one cent. I will not ask for living support from him, even though I was entitled to it. We went to *his* lawyers for me to sign that agreement, which Jim's lawyer drafted.

Normally, each party in a divorce would have their own lawyer to ensure that they were fairly treated in a settlement. Because I was not asking for anything, I chose not to have a lawyer, I left it all up to Jim. A few years later, one of my girl friends told me of her divorce story. In fact, she told me many times. She worked in the fashion industry. She loved her job but it offered little income. Her husband, to be more accurate, her ex-husband, was a real estate agent. He did very well, and had two houses. But her expensive taste was larger than her husband's. Wanting to study further, her husband gave up his job and became a post-graduate student, without income. She had an affair and then asked her husband for a divorce. In doing so, she demanded a share of their assets. I was surprised by how calmly she described all of this. It seems that my girl friend felt no guilt over her demands. German law would support her in her demands, even though she committed adultery, and that it was her who wanted the divorce.

Because I decided to leave Jim, to retain a clear conscious, and sticking to my principles, unlike my girl friend, I left it all with Jim. However, if Jim passed away, I would be the first beneficiary. I did not want to be the first beneficiary because this would be as a result of his death.

When we came out of the lawyer's office, I felt heartache, but relief. I came to Germany, with nothing, and now, I had nothing, apart from the baby in my belly.

Fate though, is a funny animal, which impinges on the future. Often, when people look back to past decisions, they would see that those decisions were probably not decisions that they would make, as fate played its own cards.

Then, from one night of love, I became pregnant. The baby was no accident, it was my decision. Irrespective of the decision being right or wrong, it was my decision to make and I would take the responsibly for the outcome – whatever the costs. I had no choice but to divorce Jim.

Christmas day, in the year 2000, I have all kinds of tubes attached to my body. I look around the hospital ward, I was alive. How many times did I dream of having a white Christmas? Now I have it – a white ward, white bed, the corridor is white, the pine trees outside of the window are all covered in snow, layer after layer. There is only one patient, me. I am peaceful, both in my body and heart, and do not even notice my breath. I have always lived with passion but now I am so quiet, because of the cancer.

For too long now I have been too passive, to try and please people. I want to strive to be more positive. In my early days, my efforts must have had some effect as I had admiration from people. Starting from my primary school days, I always came first in the class, and so was admired. However, because my parents were born in a lower class, we had no status, and so I never received *The Young Red Child's* award. I moaned to my parents, feeling that I was not good enough. This urged me to keep striving. In my high school, I still took the first place for the entire school. When I graduated from high school, the prestigious Beijing University accepted me. I was so excited. But at that stage, my parents suffered enough through the ten year Cultural Revolution because of their cultural group. I was also impacted by this and was afraid that if I chose a major in art, I would be criticised as well. I became passive. My parents wanted me to choose my major in civil engineering. Again I was passive, and did not study my preferred subject. After I graduated from university I did choose the major I wanted in a post-graduate institute. For this, I came to Germany as an overseas student. But my self-esteem was low, and unjustly I felt like a second class citizen. I became passive again. I worked hard and received top marks for my Ph.D. degree. Yet, I found it hard to find a job in Germany. I found my German prince, Jim. Our romantic love moved me with excitement, but in our day to day relationship too often I was passive. Passivity is based in Chinese culture, it's called "Xiao Shun – listen and obey to parents". For example, I was not born into a family of status, so it was expected of us to be passive. Even though I am a strong woman, too many times we have a weak side.

Before Christmas, there was only one other patient in the ward, Mrs. Web; she was seventy-six. On Christmas Eve, her children took her home for Christmas day. When Christmas, she returned to the ward.

After my operation, I was pushed into the ICU under observation for three days. After my situation stabilised, I was moved to the ward, where Mrs. Web and I greeted each other. After a couple of days we were more familiar with each other and chatted. Mrs. Web's skin was white with pink blotches. She had silver hair and eyebrows. She was easy going.

I did not expect that this old woman's life experience would became our prime topic. Before Christmas, I had friends come to visit me most days, but no one came to see Mrs. Web. I asked her if she had children. She chuckled, and used her fingers to indicate, "I have two sons, and one daughter. My eldest son is fifty-six. All three married young. Some of my grandchildren also married young, so I already have seven great-grandchildren."

"Why don't they come to see you?" I asked with confusion.

"They have to work. My sons and daughters come to see me on weekends". Mrs. Web seemed peaceful and satisfied.

"But what about your grandchildren and great-grandchildren? Do they come to see you as well?" I started to imagine the happy situation of her being surrounded by children, grandchildren, and great-grandchildren. But she shook her hand as if to cancel that idea, "I don't want my grandchildren to come, it's too much for them. They have their own lives, with their own children and work".

Cycling around Lake Constance on bicycle, Jim ordered spaghetti Bolognese for us. Whilst waiting, Jim and Tantan drink a large glass Coca-Cola.

I felt sorry for her, and was worried that she would pass away because of her sickness and age. "What about your husband?"

"We divorced ten years ago... I live by myself". She answered without hesitation and continued, "My ex-husband had a car accident afterwards and now lives in a nursing home".

I was shocked. We were silent for a while, but I could not hold my curiosity, and so asked, "Mrs. Web, you have so many children, grandchildren, great-grandchildren. This is a very happy thing. In China, we call these four-generations in one family... So... so why did you divorce?"

Mrs. Web hid nothing, "My ex-husband is not my children's father. I gave birth to my first three children from another man, but he left, when the youngest was only one and half year's old".

"Why?" I had to ask.

"I don't know. Perhaps he suddenly lost the interest in family life. People do things like that when they are young. And if I asked him now, being old, he probably could still not tell the reason... Yes, we do some silly things when we are young. My partner left, but I could not. I had three children that depended on me for survival. Then after, it was hard to find another man. Which man is willing to marry someone with three children? But as my children grew up, I met this man and we married. He was divorced as well and had his own children who lived with his ex-wife".

I still could not shut up, "So why this divorce again? That was ten years ago, you must have been sixty-five". Mrs. Web was calm when she said, "My second husband was good when he worked, and treated me and my family well. He worked and I did the housework and cooking. Our life was good. But when he retired, he became strange. He didn't know what to do with his time. At that time, I got a part-time job, but I still had to do all the housework. I was so busy, but he would not help. Not only that, he was always dissatisfied and moaned all the time. So I separated from him. I never regretted this. It felt good to be living by myself".

After I heard her story, my heart was heavy. I felt sad, hopeless, and fearful. Now, in my middle years, and with a child, I yearned for a stable family. What would my life be if I recovered? I wanted to love and be loved.

When people are young, with so much going on for themselves, they have less need of others. When getting old, they tend to be drawn to others. Separation needs conditions as well. In Germany, you can meet these conditions. Older couples need to have their own independent space when they separate.

In China, we admire the situation where a young couple commit to holding each other's hands throughout life, getting old together. When young, when we promised, "We do", we hand our life to the other, we will love until death.

I do not know how many twists and turns there are in a person's long-life journey. Because of these we change, both change. To accept this change, you need to have power and strength. Now, I have my son, my son is still very young, while his parents are getting older. He gives me responsibilities and meaning to my life. Love, I will keep on loving my love ones, such as my parents, friends, as this is meaningful. I won't though become passive again to maintain just because of love.

I was thinking while I was lying in my hospital bed, do people gain greater humility as they age? Once I was in Schonbrunn Palace, Vienna, Austria, as part of an audience tour of the life story of Francis Joseph I, and the Princess Sissi. The story impressed me greatly. There was one room that stood out for me even more. This was towards the end and only had a single bed in it. It was for Francis Joseph in his old age. Apparently, when young, he liked the army barracks life and the single bed of the soldier. When old, he missed those years as a young man in the Army.

Mrs. Web did not hide any of her life to me. She accepted the fate that was placed on her path, she lived for now, at this moment. She was a strong woman. First, she had surgery on her knee, but when running the normal tests, the doctor found that she had problem with her intestines, so again they operated. At seventy-six, with two big surgeries, she survived well.

It was not long, that with the assistance of a wheelchair to support her, she practiced walking. She was optimistic, and smiled all day, even though she came from a poor background. I was concerned about her ability to escape poverty, and asked if she shared her ex-husband's retirement fund. She did not answer me directly, but said, "I have my own retirement fund. When I was young, I was unable to work. But when my children grew up, I could work, and I did. It was too late though, and so my retirement fund is very low, at only 600 marks a month".

Shocked, I blurted out, "How do you survive on only 600 marks a month?" She replied, "There are ways… the government offers allowances. They give me funds towards my rent. I rent a one-bedroom house, the rent is 580 marks per month, and the government contributes

330 Marks towards it. I bank 250 Marks for my retirement funds, and still have 400 Marks per month for living, this is enough. I also get clothing allowances twice a year, in the spring and autumn. What else do I need?"

It seemed to me that Mrs. Web had the right attitude, and was satisfied. Even though her food was basic, or she was unlikely to be able to afford to eat out. On her bedside table was a bottle of mineral water – every time when her meal was bought to her she was offered a new bottle but she always said, "No need, I am used to tap water, please just give me tap water".

When I compare myself with Mrs. Web, I have no reason to complain about my fate.

The first time Jim visited me, I was in ICU. His cold tears woke me up. In my dazed mind, I saw a bunch of flowers swirl in front of my eyes. On his next visit, with another bunch of flowers, I could sit up. I wanted to read and so Jim brought a book for me. It was in his coat pocket. It was, *My Whole Life,* written by Marcel Lacy Lanitzki, who is a Jew. I was attracted to the book as I was concerned about the Jews who were in the Nazi Camps.

Often a nurse would come to ask me if I wanted a painkiller. So absorbed in the book I shook my head and continued reading. Many Jews were brave and survived to finally walk out of the camps – can I walk out of this hospital, walk out the cancer? I said nothing to anyone, but I had confidence in my heart. If I was determined, I would do it. Concentrated, look after myself in my recovery. In my determination, my wound from the surgery recovered quickly. On 30th December 2000, twelve days after my massive surgery, with my wound still raw, I asked the doctors if I could go home. They agreed. I did not spend Christmas at home, but was determined to spend the New Years at home.

On the 31st December, Mr Dayun Jiang, who is the Dean for overseas Chinese student services called me. He knew of my cancer. Gently he asked, "Are you out of hospital? Can you walk? If so, we invite you to come the embassy to attend our New Year's Eve concert. If you can make it, I will meet you at the door". Deep gratitude welled in my heart. I lightly made my face up, dressed for the concert, called a taxi, and went to the embassy. It felt strange being there. Many acquaintances asked me, "Mei, are you okay? You don't look well. You have lost so much weight".

Throughout the concert, sitting on a hard chair for two hours, I had to endure my wound, but I hid this well.

On 29th April 2001, Sunday, Biqing come from Switzerland. She is an excellent cello player who was born in Taiwan. We had coffee and enjoyed a beautiful afternoon together. We talked about music. Suddenly, I felt a terrible pain in my stomach that became more acute as time went on. I said goodbye to Biqing earlier than we both hoped. As soon as I got home, I bent into a ball, sweating all over my body. My parents had no choice but to urge me to go hospital. I did not want go, and they do not speak German, so could not call the hospital. Luckily though, Jim arrived. He took one look at me and called a taxi, which took me to the hospital.

It was quiet in the hospital, because it was a holiday weekend for Labour Day on 1st May. A lot of the doctors and patients were away. The pain was ongoing, and I rolled off the bed and onto the floor. The female doctor on duty helped me back into bed. She placed an injection tube into me and injected a painkiller and sedative. She had no idea as to why I was in pain. I was rendered unconscious for two days. Finally, the doctors determined that it was congestion of the colon. This apparently can be a side effect of radiation therapy. The doctor persuaded me to undergo an operation, he was firm when he said, "This has nothing to do with the cancer you had. Your tumours were removed… there is no sign of it returning. This congestion of colon causes the bloating. Once it has been put right, there won't be recurrences. But you must have surgery, because if you don't the rectum will burst, germs will proliferate… that could be catastrophic". German doctors are usually direct and I needed no further convincing, and so in a daze I signed for the procedure.

My normal doctor was at home for the holiday weekend, but once he received a notice from the hospital he returned. However, before the surgery, the doctor on duty said my situation had not worsened. And on their rounds, whilst having my rectum washed, I heard the doctors talk amongst themselves in low voices. They suggested that my rectum may settle. I heard that there was the hope. I was reluctant to have another operation, but I do not want to endure the pain again. Based on what I heard, I refused to go to the surgery. My doctor was annoyed and went back home. On the third day, I was no better, so again I signed the agreement for the operation.

For the third time in only six months, I was placed in white theatre cloths and pushed into the operation room. I had a full anesthetic. But I woke up – the God of fate gave me life, again. After this third operation, I was exhausted and with not one ounce of strength to call on. Daily, the nursing staff had to help me turn over to wash my body. Even though this was excruciating, I limited the painkillers as I wanted to use my brain and be creative. The medical staff kept saying, "Ms. Mei, you don't need to endure the pain, you are allowed to more pain killers".

It would seem that I have a strong ability for endurance, and the more I endured and resisted the pain, the more my spirit rose.

Before these latest troubles, I had bought a plane ticket to return to China at the beginning of May. I missed China so much. In July, the Shanghai Chinese Art School, and Shanghai Aiyue Accordion group were to come to Berlin to perform. I had organised the British Gardens for the venue. I was to perform with them doing what I enjoy, which really excited me.

In my hospital bed, I told my assistant how beautiful it would be to perform at the British Gardens. So engrossed, I forgot to drink water and suddenly felt faint. I was weak with nausea, my mouth and lips were dry, I battled to breathe, and there was dark in front of my eyes. I indicated to my assistant to give me water. After a time, I improved and continued our meeting.

I delayed my flight until the beginning of June, and only six months after my first operation, not even a month after my third, I boarded the Lufthansa German Airline bound for China. Once in my seat, I saw the plane was almost full, but was delighted as both seats beside me were empty. I was grateful as it allowed me to ease the pain by stretching out.

After we landed, I immediately went to the Shanghai Chinese Art School to see the principal. Although jet-lagged, I improved how I felt and looked by applying makeup on the way.

In 2000, during the time Germany held the World Expo, Beijing's Huiwen High school choir returned. Apart from arranging their performing on stage of World Expo, I looked for other things the students could do. Occasionally, I contacted the English Gardens' Jazz Group, and the organiser of the World Music Festival. In the short period left, it was going to be difficult to arrange much for the choir. When the students arrived at the British Gardens, they were impressed by the beauty, they felt that they were doomed to perform their songs here because their songs were as beautiful as the Garden.

Some students stood on the stair steps of the garden. It was such a large audience, and after the performance, some of female students had tears in their eyes. I asked them why were they crying as they had not sung any sad songs. They answered, "We are just so excited, and touched, because we sang Schubert's *The Trout* with the German audience standing and singing in beautiful harmony. Then they applauded us for so long. We never had such applause when we performed in China. The experience is unforgettable, and we will remember it for our entire life". When I heard this, I also burst into tears as I was also pleased for them to have had this experience.

On the morning of the performance, I liaised with the Berlin Multi-Culture Broadcasting Station for a recoding and interview. It was the first time that the students and their parents had been in a professional broadcasting station. During the broadcast, I, with the host, in between songs, spoke of our Chinese musical history, and of some of our traditional instruments. At the end, our afternoon's performance time and venue was announced. Upon leaving the station, the director of the broadcast station gave every student a pen as a souvenir. He handed over a CD of the broadcast performance.

I do believe that the love of life, love of work, and love of art, was to be the power that would help me recover from cancer.

JIM

After the cancer, I was unable to give birth again. And, I wanted to go back China.

Jim made me sign the agreement. I cannot really remember much of what was in it as German is not my native language. I started to learn German with gusto when I was twenty-five. After finishing my Ph.D. I did some writing in German. My writing made my father-in-law, the professor, who can speak eight foreign languages, so excited that he read it aloud to everyone. He congratulated me and said that I write better than many Germans. But for complicated German documents, I get a headache trying to understand them.

There was one day, before all the separation issues. when I bought a dining table at a furniture show. After browsing for a while, I found this discounted dining table in a dark corner. It was wood and had been used for over twenty years. Yet, the table surface was still smooth because of the good wood used. On that table there had been placed all kinds of carefully cooked meals, meals that had brought a family happiness. But at that moment, the separation agreement laid on it. I felt heartache when I saw it, with fear in my tears. I felt helpless and was too proud to read it. That is when I held my breath and signed it. Later, Jim did not want to go through with the divorce but fate had walked in front of me. In the end, I divorced Jim, because I wanted a baby.

The father is Chinese. The decision was mine. When I told Jim I was pregnant, and to a Chinese man, he broke many plates and threw things against the walls. I was afraid that his constant anger might hurt the baby in my belly, so in order to avoid fighting with him, I moved out of our home. By following my dreams, passion and capabilities, within time, I owned a bigger, and more luxurious home. Although I enjoyed this new house, and still did a lot of refurbishing myself, I did not climb ladders to paint walls, or drive a large van all over the city to carry furniture any more.

There were still some things we needed to discuss. One night I phoned him and when he heard it was me, he said, "Mei, Mei". He spoke my name in the same intimate fashion as he had for our seven years together. It was always said with the trust of two people in love. I felt sorry for him and sad. I asked Jim if he was okay. "No, I am not". Then I heard muffled crying. It was Jim who forced the separation agreement. It was his decision to divorce me when it suited him. Not until he said he did not want a child, and not one with funny eyes did I wanted to break up. I felt that once I married Jim, I would never divorce him. In that moment I felt helpless, when, half-crying, he asked me, "Mei, why did you do this? I loved you for seven years, waited for you for seven years, tolerated you for seven years, grew you as a person... for seven years. I saw your progress every day, gaining maturity until you obtained success.

We separated, and then got back to each other. We would have had children... and a wonderful home. It's just because I chose work in a different city. I felt that our relationship was not stable, and that you were still immature. I said we needed to wait to have a child. But you ran away to have one... with another man. You left me forever. You broke my heart, now I have nothing... I have lost my confidence in life and work. But you... you will never find another man who understands and tolerates you as much as I did. I was absolutely loyal to you and gave you a stable life".

He went on, crying on the other end of the phone. I heard his words, without tears, but crying within. Jim's prophesy hit me – I wondered if the fate he offered, that I would not be able to find a man like Jim to love me, would hold true.

Jim said, "I don't want to see your belly. I don't want to see your child, I don't want to see the other man, never. Do you understand? You should understand. If I were to see them, I would feel that I am a loser. Do you understand? It was my effort, but others gained recognition from my perseverance".

"Jim", I said, "you will find another woman. For all these years you kept saying that I am immature, irrational. You never cared about our home, never went shopping for furniture with me, and when I bought furniture, you said I wasted money. You moaned about my studying for my Ph.D., and that I didn't earn money for the household. When I did earn money, I immediately contributed. You wanted me not to have the career that I wanted, you wanted to make me a secretary. I wanted children… you said that our child would have small and funny eyes… like me… You were afraid that I would take your children back to China. You blamed me that I married you just because I wanted to stay in Germany, I married you for love…"

He denied what I said, "I didn't have time to care for our home. I had to earn the money. I always complimented you on the things you bought for the home. Your paintings hung on our walls. You didn't earn money and I worried that you were not independent. And when you did get an income, yes, I asked you to pay rent… but I wanted to test if you love me for real…"

Life is strange, but this became the reality as I felt the baby in my belly. I kept silent.

After Jim told me of his pain and anger on that phone call, he calmed down. Occasionally he called, but each conversation was about the divorce.

"Mei, it is not necessary to get divorced now. You married me, not for the purpose of staying in Germany. I know that now. You are not interested in my assets, you did not even get a lawyer to protect what could be yours. I don't want to divorce you. My mother said that no other wife would make a home as warm as you do. She said that I would never have such good wife as you". Hearing this, I felt devastatingly sad. Why? Why only say this now? I swore in my heart that I would support Jim in love forever. I also swore to be a good daughter-in-law for the Goodhouse family. I will make my mother-in-law proud of me. I tried – now, it is too late. I cannot endure any more. I cried loudly, "It's no use to say these things anymore. I have no choice, my baby will be born soon. He is Chinese, we will go back to China…"

I am a girl who was born in the Hunan province of China. I grew up eating chillies. I learnt from my father how to swim in the Xiang River. He said I must only swim going downstream and not up stream. My father educated me to be self-dependant. China is deep in my bones.

A few years later, deep in the night, I still feel my love for Jim. My heart quivers at the thought of his pain. I lie in bed and cannot explain my actions. I do not understand human nature. When I had no job and saw the separation agreement, my fear of loss enmeshed me. All I could do was to hold my breath and sign hid damn agreement. I hid my fear of loss and pain from Jim. He never knew how I hurt. I became strong. I did what I had to do. I had the capability to start a new life, even if a new love was unsuccessful. I declared that I would live independently and raise my son.

Freedom; Hungarian Poet: Petöfi Sándor; Name of the poem is: Szabadság, Szerelem!

Freedom and love (English Version)

> Liberty and love
> These two I must have
> For love, I will
> sacrifice my life;
> For liberty, I will
> sacrifice my love.

I read the famous poem to my friends. I explained it to them. Life is precious. But love is indeed of greater value. *'If, for the sake of freedom, I must pay, I would the above give away!'* I tried to be strong inside. My female friends told me, 'You are right. Take a couple with a child, often they fight, the energy they consume, sometimes you are better on your own. We admire that you take your freedom". My Gosh, I thought, I have no way to go back. Actually, at the time I read this poem, I was feeling weak, helpless, and lonely, to the depth of my soul. In that period, fate had its hand, and I had to be successful in work and life to wash away the hurt of my dignity – the good times and love, which Jim gave in the past, did not stop our separating.

Two months before Tantan was born, on the way to the lawyer and courthouse, we made an appointment to meet on the way. I had a big belly. When seeing Jim I did not feel happiness or pride, I felt uncomfortable. Jim was defensive at first, but loosened up. Later, when we passed a traffic light, he lightly placed a hand on my tummy, as if to protect the baby. I felt guilty.

Then I remembered that once Jim shouted at me as I drove through an early red light. "Didn't you see the light was about to change to red? Are all you Chinese people like you when they drive? How could you be the mother of my children, you will kill them by going through a red light". And now he protectively touched my stomach. I would become a mother soon and have more responsibilities. I would not drive through red lights.

Before I went out that day, I fought with Yun. Like most relationships, it happened randomly, but it happened because of passion. The relationship had only been seven months, and we tried to maintain the relationship. It was difficult. Our child had not been born yet. I was not happy, I paid for my decisions. But I said nothing to Jim.

Jim and I parted later that day, with me carrying a divorce certificate. I cried loudly.

When together, Jim gave his opinion of marriage. He said that after a few years, the heart and love goes out of the relationship. Then it is more about companionship and shared things; the home, possessions, convenience, because the love adventure is only a short-term matter. The two in the relationship get over it. I listened, but never forgot. The reality – neither of us got over it. If it were, as he suggested, that the love and adventure disappeared, it would have been easier to deal with. And even though I knew that Jim had slept with dozens of women, and always had a girlfriend when we separated, yet, I still felt guilty because of my affair.

Lake Constance. A late afternoon swim, where Tantan wants to swim to the other side but it is too far. He does not want to come out of the water.

My affair was to get pregnant. I chose this. It was done with no way back. I knew it would irrevocably dissolve the relationship between Jim and me. Even pregnant, with another man's child, and after the bitterness, Jim was slow to divorce me. I took the responsibility and made it happen. I had to take responsibility for my child. I also had to be responsible for my child's father. I never wondered if my child's father would take responsibility for me, or if he would take the responsibility for our child.

A few years later, a friend of Yun and mine's, informed me that when Yun was with me, he boasted that he was also having an affair with a married German lady. Both of us were so stupid. The telling was a splash on my face. A man and a woman have different experiences when in love. Passion can exert a high cost.

A few years later, I often suggested to my girlfriends, who had children and a rocky marriage, that I thought my case was classic. A woman's decision on who to love may affect her life for just a few months or a few years. If the relationship does not work they can part company. But a woman's decision to have a child will affect her whole life. To give birth to a child is an important decision.

I also said that the decision as to whom to have a child with is much more important than who to marry. On the contrary, it is the same for men. Men should not have a child with any female, as that is likely to give them trouble. There are males who seed a child but never take responsibility for the child. There are males who are caught by the woman after the child is conceived; they are also a fool. I think I have the experience to talk about these things. But when I was in the situation, my journey of fate was so complicated.

My son Tantan was born. For the occasion, Jim bought a bunch of flowers! "Congratulations, you are now a mother". I taught him to buy me flowers, now he did not stop. He bought flowers when I became a mother, he bought flowers after my surgery…

I went to the Beijing University at sixteen; became a post-graduate student of the world renowned Professor Zhou Li at twenty. When youthful, I was told that I was nice looking, but my first lover, who was a few months younger than me, wanted me to look younger and thinner. For this, I dieted. Each day I scrutinised myself in the mirror. I was afraid of early-forming wrinkles lining my face. In youth, there were pressures. When I came to Germany, I was twenty-five. There were many German male students, in their twenties, chasing me. They thought I was a lovely, active, oriental teenage girl. From then on, I did not look at myself in the mirror, I started to enjoy life, and relax more. At that age of twenty-five, if I had remained in China I would have been a lecturer at one of the universities. I was not carefree like the German students, where money and family were always on hand. I had the pressure of life. At the time, I wished that I could have gone back to my eighteens, and re-lived them in an easier way. After living in Germany for eight or nine years, that life helped me to understand the value of being mature, whilst remaining young in spirit. I knew that the secret of being forever young was fully to live life.

WHAT IS LIVING?
HOW TO BE ALIVE?

I never seriously thought about the above questions before I left China for Germany.

From about the age of five, I remembered my parents salary, both received 45 RMB per month. Their combined salary could buy 75kg of pork every month. At the time I went to university, their total salary could buy 100kg of pork every month. When I was overseas, my parents retired. They told me, their retirement pension can still buy 100kg of pork. In my childhood, most of my neighbours were my parents› workmates, who worked in the large state owned company. All their lives were similar. A lot of families owned a sewing machine and had a bicycle or two. Some people had shiny watches – if not, the money was saved. The breakfast for the kids of those families was rice, usually left over from the previous day and soaked in soy sauce. Those children went to school together. In our home, we had a sewing machine. For festivals or special days, my father tailored clothes, and my mother sewed them up. We would have new clothes to wear. But we did not have bicycles. My parents walked to work everyday. Before they went to work, Mum cooked us a noodle soup or egg noodle soup, then we went to school. My parents did not have shiny watches, but we had a phonograph. Not only was it shiny, it played beautiful music. Children from all around the area came to our home to listen to it. When I was accepted into university, my parents bought me a watch. I was the first in my family to have one.

At university, it seemed that most of the students wore similar clothes, and used similar things. When I went to the postgraduate institute for my master degree, all the post-graduate students received a small study allowance, paid by the government.

Arriving in Germany for study, the western life that I had read about and seen in movies became a reality; life was very different. The female teacher who taught German wore a different outfit every day. Every day her jewellery was different; she conveyed a different image every day. I changed my top daily as well, but my jeans and coat were always the same.

I hitchhiked to get to studies. A few time I stopped luxury cars, the speed was up to 220km on the Autobarn (highway), but the cars were steady, like a stone. The drivers were always calm. The maximum speed is 260km.

One Christmas, I was invited to one of my professor's home, a small house. Yet, I felt that the chandelier in their living room was no different from the chandelier in the Versailles Palace.

When I arrived in Germany, I used to collect items left on the street. On rubbish day, unwanted furniture was put on the street for trucks to pick them up. On those days, I would ride on a bicycle along the street scanning for items. It did not take too long, and I had a 17-inch colour TV. When back in the dormitory, I connected it to the electricity and it worked perfectly. It was a bit old and grubby, but I was happy.

In the bicycle shed of the student dormitory, there were old bicycles that had missing components. Some enthusiastic boys collected several and made up one that could be ridden.

Although life was very different in Germany, even though a student, I still started to work to earn money. I was not the poorest of the students. Later, I fell in love with Jim, who had a good income, and a good family. By being with Jim, I had less need to be concerned about finances. This separated me from the reality of life.

In China, after graduating, I was allocated a job by the Government. I could not choose the job. They chose for me. The good thing is that I went to a major I liked at my postgraduate institute. After it, I worked for a year at a foreign magazine publishing house. This consisted of a weekly meeting, collecting articles for each monthly issue, publishing and advertising a special issue once a year. For this job, I earned ten times more than the other people in the advertising department.

It was this money that I earned to buy my first plane ticket to Germany. I expected a Western prince to come into my life, to be fabulously in love... I married Jim. Jim had a wonderful education; since a child, he can speak, English, German, Italian, and Spanish etc. Seven languages in total. He read novels in all these languages, he even wrote a novel. But he did not study literature, nor language. His major was in civil engineering. Why engineering? It was purely for a career path – the belief is that you should have a job first.

I obtained my Ph.D. but I did not have a job. I was not in a hurry to find a job. I started to write a monograph per an invitation from China. China paid my draft fee, which I exchanged for German marks. From this I bought a return plane ticket to and from China. I dreamt of establishing a cross-culture, China-German, institution. I did not need go to work but just to have this daily dream. Jim said, "If you study civil engineering, you would have a job. But you studied art. An art degree won't give you employment in Germany... where are you going to find a job?"

In Germany, the history of Art, and art related majors, are called 'unemployment majors'. After graduation, many of the students cannot find a job. For me, being Chinese made it even harder. In Germany, art related majors are also called 'the rich wife's major'. Because of the subjects in art majors, many females become more accomplished, and perhaps more able to be a rich wife. I became a wealthy man's wife, but never with the idea of sitting back and doing nothing. If it was not for the economic downturn, Jim would not have cared if I had a job. I published a Chinese monograph, and Jim was proud of me. The travel costs for me to fly back to China were paid by Jim. I gave my draft fees to my parents. With the downturn, because of Jim's upbringing, he did not know how to cope with the risk, how to face the possible unemployment.

After I separated from Jim, I did not write monographs any more. I gave up my dream to establish a cross-cultural institute. I was not a housewife who was supported by a husband any more. I looked for a job everywhere in Berlin. It did not take too long and I found a job with the international training company.

It gave me a good income. But it was not satisfying. All that was in my mind were art ideas, which were related to China. I used my holidays to lecture in China. There were people in the same industry who invited me to open an art exhibition. After the exhibition, I would travel to Europe to look around, to support my dream. At the beginning, I partnered with a German company. I was paid a salary so the compliments were credited to the company. I became independent after a while. I not only did art exhibitions, but created the China-German Art Festival, as per my dream.

I started my career and felt that I shouldered all the responsibilities well. Then the cancer came, as did the various surgeries. Work, work and work, I thought of my work even when I was lying on the hospital bed. Am I a workaholic because I like my work? I must work. I need the income. I overcame the pain caused by Yun and my sister.

Once married to Jim, I did not follow the German custom of changing my surname to that of my husband's. I kept my surname, as per Chinese custom. In Germany because my husband's surname is Goodhouse, I was normally addressed Mrs. Goodhouse. I was not really used to it. But as time went by, I adjusted to be a Mrs. Goodhouse, I tried to announce myself as Mrs. Goodhouse. I found, especially on phone calls, when a German person called me Mrs. Goodhouse, it was easier for me as they were more helpful.

After the divorce, I had to use my Chinese name for everything. It was very difficult as I felt that my separation with this country became bigger. After our break up, the cancer and other issues became my fate. Fate though, should not interfere with a person's responsibilities, unless you give up. Sometimes responsibilities overwhelm people. I do not want to die, I want to live, and if that means taking responsibility that is okay. To be alive is the initial motivation for me to have my own dreams.

With my early study in Beijing, then all the time in Germany, I did not share the Chinese New Year with my parents. It seemed to them that I did not care about this. However, it was difficult at the time, but now in my middle age I do realise that it is important to me. Twelve years ago, when my parents came to Germany to take care of me, it was the sickness that enabled our reunion – I returned to my parents' hug. At the time, when they stayed in Germany to looked after me, news came from China that they had finally been allocated a house to purchase. A new house, if they had the money. Over the years of my being away, my motherland had changed massively. So at last, my parents could finally purchase a new house, and I could help them. I gave them the money that I had saved for my own house in Germany so they could get a beautiful house. They now have the house, but the nicest thing is that my parents are still healthy and can enjoy life. They deserve this in their old age. They worked hard all their life. I want them to be happy and to rest in their old age, without any worries. I did not want to die before they could enjoy this life. In fact, this was another motivation for me to stay alive and gain health, so I could help them. I remember the time when I married Jim, I was stingy and did not pay for trips for them to travel to Europe. Now, I hope that because of me, my parents' will be like German elders, and travel all over the place.

JIM AND TANTAN

In Germany, like anywhere in the West, to get married or to divorce, is decided by the couple. It does not matter if it is a good or bad relationship, no one would interfere, all minding their own business. But when a woman becomes a mother, she receives a lot of advice from everyone. They praise you for the new life. They encourage you to take responsibility. They pray for you to enjoy the happiness of raising your child. When walking the child in a pram or whilst holding the child in a shopping centre, you receive smiling glances and encouragement from strangers. Some offer to help. I loved being a mother, even though the rest of my life was troublesome. Being a mother was a happy event for me. It was not until Tantan was one year old, when his father left, when I was told I had cancer, that it was Jim who was with me.

Jim was worried, not just for me, "When you are in the hospital, what will happen to Tantan? I have to work. Perhaps you must put him in an orphanage or give him to welfare". Jim started to search for an orphanage or welfare house. I was deeply hurt, "Jim, you don't need to help me. I don't want you to help me. My son won't go to an orphanage or welfare".

When I think of this situation, it makes me sad. Yes, I lived with Jim for seven years. I dreamt of having a child with him. Now I have a child, but it is not Jim's. To fulfil my promise to my life, for my son, for my son's father, with tears, I divorced Jim. By doing so, I lost my only dependency in Germany. After the surgery, in that big city, which is not my hometown, I only have my ex-husband, Jim, who is not my son's father, to be with me.

After I came out of hospital, Jim often visited me. He always brought flowers. Tantan smiled when Jim comes, he shouted, "Jim, Jim". Jim would ask, "How are you young man?" then Jim would say to Tantan, "These flowers are for Mum… Mum likes flowers". Tantan would cling to

Jim. He loved riding on Jim's shoulder, where he would become taller than Jim. Jim played magic games with him. Another game Tantan loved was when Jim would raise his middle finger for Tantan to grab, but just before he got it, Jim would bend and hide the finger. Tantan would scream and laugh loudly as he tried to find Jim's finger all over the house. Sometimes, Jim would grab a grass root from outside, and hold the grass as if it was the middle finger. Jim would nonchalantly whistled a tune, and Tantan would rush to Jim and try to grab the grass from him. Tantan also tried to whistle the tune but he could not. Jim would say, "Oh, you want to whistle my tune, let's learn how to play it on the piano".

This was my wish for Tantan. After I moved into this big apartment, one of the first thing I did was to buy a piano, the same as Jim's. Now, when Jim visits I can still enjoy his piano playing. I wanted Tantan to learn how to play the piano. When Tantan was in my belly, I played piano for him every day. I only can play a few simple tunes. Tantan watched Jim closely when he played. A bad habit developed, where the playing delayed his dinner time. Jim always laughed and didn't care. But when I nagged, he said to Tantan "Okay, little one, we should eat dinner, then we can play again. If Mum is upset, that will affect her health, and that's not good".

Seeing Jim with Tantan, how patient he was, and how he spoilt him, I would give a deep sigh of regret. Before we separated, when I chatted with Jim about fatherhood, I praised his good temperament for children and said he would be a good father. When Jim played with his sister's kids, he was a good uncle. But Jim always said that he thought he would be annoyed by his own children. He would say not to expect him to play with his children. Those words poured cold water on my dreams of having a child with him. Tantan is not his child, but he treated him with much more patience than I did.

BOGELT

Jim and I were not a couple anymore. Because of the cancer, our relationship became close again. We had unlimited trust between us. When Jim visited me, sometimes he talked about his women. He met one in a bar, and met another in a disco. None of these girls seemed to last long, until the autumn of 2002, when he had a longer-term girlfriend, Bogelt. He told me she was young, a medical student, very clever. Soon she would graduate, and was practicing in a hospital. I do not remember if Jim told me about Bogelt's character or hobbies, but I remember he said that "Bogelt isn't like you, she is self-contained. She's humble and loves me a lot. We went to the cinema one night; being a student, she has little money. She doesn't want to buy drinks or popcorn as they are expensive in the cinema. She brought two bottles of beers from a supermarket, as they are cheaper there. She knows that I like beer".

When Jim told me these things, to him it seemed that he was chatting of trivialities. He held no emotion in his voice. Only Chinese can make Jim's voice with low or high tones (in Chinese, there are four different tones, where each tone can express different feelings). When Jim spoke in German, he only had one tone. Frustrated, I demonstrated, "Jim, you are so foolish, what are you waiting for? Such a good girl, you should marry her soon. If you let her go, you won't find another like her". But Jim mumbled, "Bogelt hopes that I would love her... she wants me to say I love her, and forever. But I told her I don't know what love is. I won't say I love anyone anymore. If she loves me too much, I will leave her, because I only can hurt her. Look at what happened to us? Everyday, and several times, you always told me that you loved. I would say I love you several times a day. But I felt a bit strange, I swallowed them." But I had a good feeling to unknown Bogelt, somehow.

Not long after, one night, when brushing my teeth, there was bleeding. Since the cancer, I was terrified every time I saw my blood. I called

Jim immediately and told him. He told me that he was with Bogelt and that I must go to the hospital by myself. I said I did not want to go. Twenty minutes later, my doorbell rang. Jim rushed in, "Come, you are going to hospital straight away", and practically dragged me into the taxi. After checking me out for half a day, nothing was wrong. When we came out of the hospital, I apologised about his date with Bogelt. He said, "I told Bogelt, and being a doctor she understands. She even told me to accompany you". I had a good feeling about the unknown Bogelt.

Later, I held a party at my home. I invited many people. I especially invited Jim and asked him to bring Bogelt. When they came, I wanted to chat with Bogelt and get to know her. But there was no easy opportunity. So many guests came and went. Most of the guests were in the lounge room. Bogelt stayed in the kitchen with some other guests. I did not interfere.

What did I want to tell Bogelt? Actually, there might be nothing I could say or to tell her. I have good feelings towards her from what I heard from Jim, and what I saw of her I liked. She was strongly independent, as many modern German girls are. Tall and slim, very young. She smoked cigarette after cigarette. I felt that there was no way to communicate with this type of German girl. On the surface, their independence looks fine, but it stops them from receiving help or friendship from another. They do not know how to support their German men; she is unlikely to be able to support Jim. But on their inside, there is no doubt that they need love from men. I have a girlfriend, Linda. She is an excellent choir director. When she is on stage, she is charming, and has the respect of the whole team. Once she is off the stage, the members would say that Linda does not make eye contact and keep people at arm's length. Linda would sit opposite me when we had a meal together. She would ask, "Mei, what can you tell from looking into my eyes?" German males always miss those type of German females, they would turn to women of other countries who are softer.

Actually, I want Bogelt to become a German me. I want Jim to marry her quickly and that they have children. I want Jim to be happy. They could have a good life together. Jim would not think that Bogelt only married him for the purpose of staying in Germany.

But Bogelt is not me, I am not Bogelt.

Reflections, love until death | 187

Jim and Bogelt broke up. He said, "Bogelt told me that I must be seeing another woman as I do not love her. Women are so strange, I don't have other women. She won't allow me to see her. But in her heart, she's waiting me to go to her. I did go after her, but repeating this game is not fun".

Hearing this, I knew that Jim was repeating things he did in the past. He often said that, before me his relationships with other women always ended in a bad way. Women were hurt and gone. He would say, "It does not mean that I intend to hurt women". A good point though, is that he is not the type of man who wants to control. He does not dominate a relationship. When we were married, he spoilt me all the time. If it were not because of the risky economy, and the concern about his employment, Jim would have been proud of my Ph.D. He felt pride that I published my thesis. But because the major I did for the Ph.D. was art, which held few employment prospects, this was his concern. Jim never felt inferiority because he did not have a Ph.D. His love for me was genuine, which made me feel good. On the contrary, I have overcome my Chinese culture conditioning of the man having to be more qualified than the woman. Certainly, the man must at least match his wife's qualifications. At first, I felt Jim may be reluctant to be with me and I felt saddened by this.

Months later, he told me, "Bogelt left a message on my phone. She has cancer, brain cancer."

"My God, she's so young. Jim, you need to visit her". I said with real concern.

But Jim said, "No, she doesn't need me. I have no relationship with her now".

I felt that was cruel of Jim. I lowered my tone, "Jim, you should go, you must go, she needs you. Otherwise, she would not have left you that message".

Fortunately, he listened and visited her. He passed on the good news that Bogelt seemed to be getting better.

He also told me, he was about to leave Berlin for a job in Southern Germany. I felt fear deep inside. His job situation must have been bad as he did not want to leave Berlin. When he went, he kept his apartment. He returned some weekends and public holidays.

When he visited, he seldom talked about girls, and nothing about marriage. But, he did talk about having children. There was one time though, he had about a dozen pictures of different woman. He proudly showed these to me, but also a little embarrassed, "Look, all these women are interested in me. Look at this one, she is attracted to me. She even came to Berlin to see me, crazy".

I scanned these pictures with embarrassment. They are all tall and slim women. Some women reveal tool much, wearing too little, yet, they look empty inside. I thought they looked like prostitutes, but scolded myself – how could I judge these girls just by their photo?. I was too biased and I did not put too much value in any of these women for Jim. I asked in a dry voice, "What does this woman do?" He answered, "She is a trainee, an assistance to an ecologist. She came to Berlin for me. But I don't care for her, or any of these women. But I want one of them to give me a child. I would pay a surrogate fee".

When I had cancer, my doctor told me that the chemo would not affect my fertility. When they removed my rectum, they said it would be very hard, and dangerous for me, to get pregnant again. I wanted to have another child. I was not afraid to die to have this child. I had the courage to overcome all the difficulties. When the doctor who did the radiation therapy on me said that I cannot give birth to a child in the future because of the radiation, that was another big slap. I longed to give Tantan brothers and sisters. That kind of loss and pain cannot be measured. There is no higher purpose or meaning than to give birth to children. I thought about it repeatedly. I am alive and want to have children, because I love life. I thought that if one is a pessimist, then there is no meaning to life. I would not give birth to any child. But I was positive, I was given this by my parents. They had to work hard but always maintained a positive attitude towards life.

I felt sad and dizzy. Jim talked about giving birth to a child so easily now. I recalled those past discussions where he did not want to talk of having children. That afternoon, Jim played football with Tantan in the park at the zoo. They were so excited, laughing loudly. Jim must have forgotten his words to have children with other woman. There were a few times when Jim called to Tantan, "Go and call Mum to come and play with us". I was sitting far away on the grass trying to read a book. There was a picture that always came to my mind: that if Jim had a child with another woman, and if that woman went away, and Jim not could take care of the child – I would look after my son, and Jim's child. But Jim and I are not so close any more. I could only be close to his child – Jim is only close to Tantan.

LAKE CONSTANCE

I prefer not to drive on the highway when I drive in Germany. But I drove from Frankfurt to the most southern part of Germany, 500km, to visit Jim who lived beside Lake Constance. Lake Constance, and the Black Forest, are famous natural landmarks of Germany. The lake is also the border between Switzerland, Austria and Germany. The place where Jim lived was only five minutes› walk to the lake. It was stunning. Rich people have built their houses against the lake. Every house has a different architectural style. I was attracted by it. I asked Jim to find out which houses were for rent. I thought it would be fun to invite some of my friends for a holiday there. Jim laughed at me loudly, "You are too diligent, always thinking of business." I didn't mind it at all, "It's so beautiful here... I will design a bicycle track around the lake... If my friends come, I won't ask them for money, I want them here for fun. Beautiful places should be enjoyed with friends, otherwise it would be too lonely. But I will also bring wealthy people from China to come and relax. They won't mind paying a lot of money".

Jim and I walked through the small lanes around the lake area. Jim's family had visited Jim several times. Jim mumbled that his mother said his house is too messy, so she stayed in a hotel. He moaned to me, "Why couldn't my mother use the money she paid for the hotel to hire a cleaner to clean my house? It's only 100 square metres".

I looked at Jim, shocked. He told me that from when he was a small boy, until he left home, every morning his mother put the clean bed sheets on his bed. His mother cooked for him, and did everything for him. But still Jim criticised. On school holidays, she always organised activities for the children; skiing, mountain climbing, and many more. As children, she encouraged all her four children to learn piano. "I wanted to learn, but my younger sister did not. She felt that learning the piano was like taking medicine and thought it was a waste money".

I admonished Jim, "You should have more gratitude for your mother. For your entire life she has worked hard for you, and has shown you love. Furthermore, your taste of music is the result of your mother's support". Jim of course did not understand this thinking. I would have loved for my mother to push me to learn to play the piano. Jim continued complaining about his mother. He said that "She forced us to learn to ski from the age of six. Every year she sent us for lessons and skiing. When I was sixteen, I could teach kids how to ski, and earned money from it. After that, my mother didn't need to pay any of my skiing costs". He laughed when he told me this.

I remembered the time when we went to the Alps to ski. Jim complained that I was too slow, he grumbled, "You are too slow, I may as well be sleeping". So I kind of closed my eyes, handed my life over to whatever happens, and went faster. I felt happy and fearful. Jim, so excited, carried me on his back, and shouted "Fantastic, let's go again".

I do hope though that he will teach Tantan to ski. Recently, Tantan asked, "Does Jim know how to snowboard? I want to learn". My son is so cool.

While we were walking, Jim waved his long arm and I noticed a small hole in his top. Frowning, I asked him, "How come you are still wearing that old ski top I bought you? It's over ten years old". "What's wrong with it? It's good quality. It only has a small hole. I can send it away to be sewn, but it will cost about 20 Euro".

Seeing that he still liked the top I bought him, I felt warm in my heart. I said, "Don't wear it anymore, I will buy another". I didn't immediately buy a new ski top for Jim, instead, I bought him a pure wool coat. On the day I posted it to him, in a hurry I used my business title and address; 'Chairperson of xxx international communication association'. I received Jim's reply immediately as, "This is the CEO of International Skiing Club, Jim XYZ". In his reply mail, Jim teased me as a workaholic, who treated private letters to friends as official business matter. Yes, only Jim would scolded me like this, not offering the respect for a friend. I was concerned that I did not have more time for my friends and was too busy to separate my private and official matters. But it was so difficult, having to work, whilst being a single mother. I had to pay attention not to make myself too tired, as I was scared of the re-emergence of the cancer. I really had no time.

After a while, I received another correspondence from Jim, "Mei, thanks for the sweater, it is just like one I would buy, and so I wear it often". I replied, "This is not the famous German brand you like, I bought it from China as I did not want you to spend 20 Euro to have the old one sewn up. If there is a hole just let me know. I will buy you a new one".

That afternoon, it snowed lightly. We drove and appreciated the great views and the castles on the mountain. Watching the lake, and boats on the lake, we drove onto the ferry and crossed the lake to the city of Constance. After driving around the city, we went to another half island on the lake. It was so tranquil. We viewed the church, and then came back to the lakeside and talked with the birds. When we went back to the city, we decided to go into a café, where we leisurely watched the lake, whilst enjoying cake. Everything was so pretty, very tranquil. It made us forget the worries of the world. Jim, between sipping his coffee, became talkative. "I am writing to a woman".

"Why?" I asked awkwardly.

"I met her at a conference. She separated from her husband, but she hasn't divorced yet. We have swapped many letters between us. She wants to come see me. She has said this several times over the last two months, but she still has not come. I don't know if I want her to come or not".

"What else does she say in her letters? She may have separated from her husband but in view of they not being divorced, do you really want to have a relationship with her?" Of course, I was nosey.

"The separation has been for over five years now. In reality, their marriage is dead".

"Even though they have been separated for over five years but not divorced... you should not interfere in this".

"That is her problem. She's thirty-six, and divorced twice already. But she has no children. She said she has psychological problems, and almost lost her job".

"You wouldn't have a child with such a woman? She is still legally married, and you said she has psychological problems... if she got pregnant with your child....." It had been a wonderful day, but when Jim started again on the topic of children, I became annoyed. I wanted to leave him on the island.

It was fun in the city of Constance, where we encountered a carnival. It was getting towards dusk and the snow and rain had eased off. After the carnival, the crowds headed toward a bar, a restaurant, or a café. Some were dressed up, some just casual but all were filled with excitement. Each establishment had a different feel – full and noisy, many with music, others much quieter. Jim and I watched as we strolled past these with interest.

Although many were enticing, that night I thought that my own home would be the cosiest place. I said to Jim that I didn't want to dine out. I would rather cook for us. It would not matter how late it would be. I will be responsible for dinner tonight, but we needed to shop. Which we did in a supermarket. We also shopped for Jim's house as well to stock up.

When I busied myself in the kitchen, I did not ask Jim for help. He lounged against the doorframe, watching me cook. It was like many nights when we just married –

Jim came home from work, I would be busy cooking, he would lean on the doorframe, with a bottle of beer in his hand and we would chat.

When we ate, I saw the dinner service he used was still the lake-blue Danish china, which was my mother-in-law's wedding gift to us. After dinner, Jim played the piano for a while, but I was not in the mood to sing. At bedtime, I saw that the sheets were still those that I bought during our time together.

The next morning, I announced that I had to go immediately. Jim asked me awkwardly, "Can't you stay for a few more days? Don't drive the 500km back so soon". How could Jim know, that the more awkward he was, the more I wanted to escape?

The summer holidays arrived. I never heard if Jim made some woman pregnant. He did ask me to visit and bring Tantan. I told him, "I have no energy to take the ten hour train trip to listen to your boring discussions about another woman giving birth to your child". Jim assured me on the phone, "I will play with Tantan, I have no need talk about giving birth to a child".

When we arrived at Lake Constance, Tantan was excited to the point of bursting. Jim arranged for the three of us to ride bicycles around the lake. First, he took two bicycles out from the bicycle shed. Then declared, by patting the seats of the bicycles, "This one for Mum, this one is mine".

"What about mine?," asked a worried Tantan.

"Don't worry my little friend, my neighbour is a grandpa, and he has two grandsons who live in America. I borrowed one for you." Tantan immediately cheered up, "We all three have bikes now".

Jim helped Tantan to pump up the bicycle tyres. Next, the brakes were checked, helmets passed around. Jim taught Tantan how to change gears. They went out to do warm-up excises. I started to pack our lunch.

Lake Constance in summer has blue skies, puffy-white clouds, deep-green waters, and unlimited mountains. We rode our bicycles past many grape vines, and wineries. The area is famous for good wines, so when we wanted a rest, and we went into a cellar. I told Tantan that wine cellars are good for playing hide and seek. Actually, I just wanted some shade for a while. When back on the road, the vista of hills and grape vines reminded me of Chinese tea plantations – of mountainsides and terraced fields. Then I thought of the beautiful Olive groves on mountains in Italy. All of these views have some similarities but also, they have their own character.

We saw many other cyclists, and some with bags on the bike frame or backpacks of camping equipment. They were tourists, and would spend several days in the area.

At the lake, after seeing all the yachts, Tantan wanted one of his own. I promised him that "First you must grow up a bit. Then Jim will teach you so you can get a skipper's license".

All along the road, by the lake there were magnificent hotels. Also nice were all the smaller inns, which were brilliant in the sunlight. You ate there, you stayed there, you took leisure there – one day, two days, half a month. The entire area was so clean, not a paper or tin to be seen, nothing to make visitors feel uncomfortable. I took photos of each inn. Jim laughed at me, that I must be thinking of business again. I really hoped that one day I could bring Chinese people to come to enjoy this beauty. But Jim did not understand me. I did not need to do the business for myself, I just wanted to express my creative ideas for people from China.

On other days, Jim took Tantan on a boat cruise, or for ice cream, to watch street entertainers. I would wander off to the shops and look for clothes. There were some well discounted that looked good, but none satisfied me at the time. Jim would get annoyed and say, "How could you lose us?". I replied shamelessly, "Easily, I left Tantan with you, he likes you more".

When we left Lake Constance and said goodbye to Jim, I asked Tantan, "Would you like to come and visit Jim once a year, is this a good idea?" "No, once a month", Tantan answered without hesitation.

What Tantan said made me laugh, but it was hard for me to visit Jim regularly as the distance between Berlin in the south, and Lake Constance in north, was just too great.

What about Tantan? He loved Jim. Since he was three, he would say quite clearly, "Mum, my dad treats you badly, he always fights with you. Jim treats you well". But Tantan loved his dad as well.

In order to exposed him to Chinese culture, I sent Tantan back to Beijing for primary school. I did not choose a German primary school or an international school. I chose a normal Chinese public school. One close to home. When I was at high school, I gave up the expensive private schools and went to a normal public high school, close to home. I preferred to be at home with my parents and sister. I believed that this is important. I had my reasons for not seeing Tatan's father, but I could not stop Tantan from seeing him, nor his grandparents, who loved him very much.

In China, Tantan also had grandparents from my side. There were so many relatives around him. But Tantan also had close ties with Jim. Sometimes, Tantan would moan, "Mum, I miss Jim".

A YEAR END PHONE CALL

A few years after our divorce, and because of my cancer, our relationship became close again. There were times when our feelings towards each other were like when we were married. In Berlin, there was one time when we went to a movie, Jim insisted that we have dinner together. On the phone call as normal, I teased him, "Jim, as you are inviting me to dine, and a movie, I think you should pay for everything".

"Yes, I want to invite you, and I will pay for the lot".

I asked, "What makes you become so generous all of a sudden?"

For a moment, the line was quiet, until, with the sound of embarrassment, and reflection, "You... showed me how to be more generous. Do you remember when we were in Frankfurt and you were to have your driving license test? I promised you that if you passed that I would take you to dinner. But you failed. Because you failed, you were in a bad mood. I did take you to an Indian restaurant, where I wanted to order a kid's meal for you. You got even more upset. How stingy I was at that time. Now I understand more, money is not the most important thing. I am not as terrified to lose my job now as I know life will continue anyway."

I was confused on my end of the phone. Although I did not think of him to be a cheapskate, I did not tease him anymore, so I said, "Yes you have changed, you have become more relaxed... and stronger. We will enjoy the night, you don't need to pay for all. I was just teasing you".

I have the tendency to be cheeky and say things. When I put the phone down, I sunk into deep thought. When at the lake, I did not know how it started but I expressed a thought that I had harboured for a time. "Jim, you know I so wanted to have a child with you, but I did it another way. I think the cancer is my punishment".

"Don't talk nonsense" Jim reprimanded me. "Tantan is such a smart, lovely boy, you should be alive and healthily for him. Besides, you don't have cancer now, you are healthy".

I continued in another direction, "You thought I was not mature enough, and that I always went through red lights. Now you always say that you would surrogate the child of yours, no matter which woman gives it birth. I am worried about those women you mentioned, and who have so many problems. Actually, if a woman gives birth to your child, and if she won't or can't take care of the child, I will look after it. I will take care of both Tantan, and your child. I would be satisfied if I have two children".

Jim heard what I said and slowly shaking his head said, "So many years have passed, I must hurry. Tantan is so lovely, you should help me find a Chinese girlfriend".

My face was full of tears. When we divorced, Jim shouted, "Chinese women, Chinese women, I will never want a Chinese woman again". I was so sad. I knew that as only one of a billion Chinese women, that I could not be considered their representative. In those moments, I could not get rid of the feeling that I, on behalf of all Chinese women, felt humiliated. I only ever wanted to be a good wife, and a good daughter-in-law. One of the reasons why is that I wanted to show how nice Chinese women are.

Now, after all these years, after all the women he had dated, Jim was saying that he wanted to find another Chinese girlfriend, for a child! Was it because he recalled the delicious Chinese dishes I cooked? Did he miss our home life in Berlin, our home, me being on top of the shaking ladder when I painted the entire house, all by myself, and where I hung my 'immature' pictures? Every time, when my parents-in-law came to visit, they always praised our house, as it has never been so well decorated or so clean. Now that he is divorced, his house is messy, again. His mother won't stay there. Did Jim recall that on our holidays, we always went to somewhere expensive, but with an inexpensive price tag; Europe, Egypt, skiing in the Alps? It was always I who studied the best route, at the best costs. I always found the cheapest plane tickets, booked the best but the most suitable hotels. All our past, all those experiences. I did not know how to say these things to him properly in German. I replied, "You're dreaming, I would never introduce any Chinese girl to you. You've already hurt one Chinese girl. Besides, you won't find a better Chinese girl than me!"

Tantan went to Beijing for early-school. I became transient, commuting between China and Germany. I enjoyed this life. I did not visit Jim anymore. I knew that because of the cancer operations, I could not give birth again. This meant that I could not think of a relationship with Jim anymore. I kept in touch with him via phone calls and mail. A few years later, Jim told me that he had moved to Switzerland, on the other size of Constance Lake. There were a few times when I called him, and a woman answered. Jim was not there. I thought I could hear a crying child in the background. I felt dizzy and sad. I asked myself, am I not prepared for Jim to have his own children? In the deep recesses of my mind, did I still hope that Jim belonged to me, or that he did not deserve to have his own children and woman? I scolded myself, this was not right.

A few days later, when I calmed down, with determination, I called again. Thankfully, this time Jim answered. I said I called him the other day. He calmly replied, "You are wrong, I don't have a woman in my life".

Since the risk of unemployment in the mid-90s, and because of the global financial crisis, there was little civil engineering work, so Jim studied Information Systems so as to move into that field. He sent out over thirty CV's to different companies – all were rejected. He then studied job application and interview skills, so as to present himself in a more professional way.

Jim had been living at Lake Constance, which is the most beautiful and comfortable place in the world. But he felt there were better opportunities in Switzerland, and that they were more advanced in IT, so he moved from the German side of Lake Constance to the Swiss side, where he did get an interesting and well paid job.

Work or not work, he kept up his fitness routine, and every year participated in a 42.2km Marathon that went from the Swiss side to the Germany side. He also sung in two choirs, travelled a lot, skied, and bush-walked. He was active and healthy. His parents and family were well, …. I got this info from him, and glad he was well, but he said nothing about girlfriends or possible children.

On 31st December 2011, from Berlin, I called Jim, per my intuition. I phoned, not so much to celebrate the New Year, but it was also Jim's birthday. I phoned with no agenda other than to keep in contact. If Jim did not answer, I would have felt lost. But when he did, I felt even sadder. "Happy birthday. And it's New Year's Day. How are you celebrating?"

He, in a demure voice, "I am just by myself. I did not go and visit my parents".

Every time I called I felt sad. Perhaps I should not call. But I do want to get his news.

It has been a decade since we divorced, yet, I still cannot stop missing him. I miss our marriage. I even miss the painful arguments, like when he said I only married him for the purpose of staying in Germany. Because of my dignity I was hurt seriously, and so I attacked him. I still cannot understand why Jim said that. We loved each other very much. He also said that Chinese people are funny. Yet, he is friendly to all Chinese people he comes across. He studied Chinese, and Chinese history. So did his parents. All are internationally open-minded people. They have been to China several times. Every year Jim's father would invite Chinese professionals to come to visit his institution. I still follow Jim's father's notoriety – in China, over ten thousand miles away I often read in professional magazines about Jim's father. The latest was when he was congratulated on his seventieth birthday. I still recall with fondness the time when Jim's father read my German language Ph.D. essay preface, and how excited he was. Both his parents praised me, but never did Jim praised me. Realistically, I knew that my German was not better than most academic Germans. But my Chinese is excellent. I think in Chinese, and transform it into German. That would make my German different from correct German.

After our divorce, Jim wanted me to remain in Germany. He hoped that my son would stay in Germany.

What about me? In Germany, I had my German passport, a good job and a lovely house. But these were not my reasons for staying in Germany. What was my *real* motivation for staying in Germany? To me, love is the only motivation. Love is the anchor, especially when I was in my youth.

THE DIARY

My dear child Tantan,

Your mum is now thirty-four years old. When I was to be your mother, according to my German doctor, I was already older than the average gestation age of German women. The doctor said, "From now on the deformity rate of the embryo increases with each year". Mom panicked. I prayed that it was not necessary for you to be pretty, but I prayed for your health.

Nowadays, my little rabbit, I found, because of you, a rebirth. I hope that one day, that you will grow up with my smile, later my wrinkles. This thought makes me happy. It is you who makes my life rich, and forever young.

When I passed my thirtieth birthday, suddenly, I could not help but stare at the other people's children, a warmth would rise up from the depth of my heart when I did. After graduating with my Ph.D., I started to work. I suddenly had tension, I was afraid that after ten years of study and work that had passed so quick, I would miss the chance to give birth to a child – you entered my life at the time I was so firm on wanting a child. Your mum wanted a son. It seemed that you sensed that, and you became my son.

I want to tell you that in my thirty-four years of life, there was never such a strong desire to obtain anything, but to create you. I devoted myself thoroughly to you. It's an incomparable feeling when I decided to create, and nurture another life. My blood boiled with need.

My dear child, when your mum was born, she lived in a sixteen square metres hut with your aunty, and grandparents – together, all four of us. Now you are about to be born; Mum will find a bigger house for you. She will give you your own bedroom, which will allow you to play freely. I am already dreaming of you in your cradle, besides my bed.

I will watch you sleep, sweetly. If you feel lonely, you have the right to cry, or scream, if you will. I will be there to hug you, comfort you, hold you, fed you and play with you. However, you should understand, you will not be spoilt. You are not a little emperor. I have already start to design your room, it will be colourful for you.

My dear child, I do not know if you would inherit your mum's genes of travelling by herself. It is a life experience, one that you will never regret. It can be lonely. Different cultures, different people, animals and nature that seem strange to us, but all of interest and teach. Whenever I returned, I was refreshed. At first, when I arrived in Germany, Mum went to many large cities, as well as small towns. I learnt of the German customs. I even wanted to write a book on German customs. I have been to many European countries, as well as Egypt and America.

I hoped to take you somewhere before you were born. At first, I could not as my life wasn't settled. When we settled into a new house, at seven months pregnant, I took the chance, when your father was away on business. I went to a travel agent, and booked for Turkey, for four days in Istanbul. After I arrived home, I received a phone call from the agent, where he said, "Sorry madam, I forgot that you are pregnant. When you are over twenty-eight weeks you require a doctor's certificate to allow you to fly." That was a Friday afternoon. I tried to see my obstetrician but he could not fit me in for an appointment. With rising worry, I called another doctor's clinic. She said she would have to do a thorough check up on me first, only then could she determine if it was safe for travel. The thought of a check-up scared me, as already there were some negative conditions, for example, my hemoglobin level was low. When I did have the check-up, Mum's hemoglobin level was only 8.6, where it should be around 11. The new doctor gave me an iron injection, and advised Mum to start using iron supplements. In the end, she gave us permission to travel, and the certificate.

After we arrived home that night, Mum called a few friends. One of the friends said that I should not go at this time. She tried to persuaded me to cancel the travel, and stay in bed to rest. Pregnancy is not easy, and a black cloud overwhelmed me – fear rose from inside. Should I go to Istanbul? I hesitated, especially because you were in Mum's belly. But if I did not go, Mum would feel trapped, and would rather die. Going would invigorate me.

The next day we went. The most important time for a pregnant woman on a flight, is the take off and the landing. At normal times of flying, I would feel dizzy upon landing or take off. But at this time, I placed my concentration on touching you so you would not be fearful. After all, you must experience this with your full heart as well. The amazing thing was that on this flight, I didn't feel not one bit dizzy.

In Istanbul, Mum was touched by the Muslim culture. There were so many mosques, more than churches in Europe. You and I went on a ferry and travelled from the continent of Asia to the continent of Europe. We took a bus and went to a strange small towns, to see how the Turks live, and to learn some of their culture. All the time, Mum kept touching you, placing her hand on her belly. I told you story after story. We received many friendly greetings from Turkish people. We tasted all kinds of Turkish foods, and sweets. Mum totally forgot about not being strong enough.

On the flight on the way back, Mum kept mumbling, "Istanbul… Istanbul". At that time you had not received your name. My mumbling, "Ist… Ist". Pronouncing the second syllable, "Stan…stan, and then bul…bul". When the flight landed safely, suddenly your name came. You would be named SiTan. Si in Chinese Mandarin means thought, Tan in Chinese means undisturbed. Is it not a good name?

Later, I consulted a Turkish friend, "Stan" in Turkish means "king". In German and English, "Stan" is also a male name. Dear Tantan, I chose "Si", with the Chinese meaning to encourage you to be diligent in thought, and "Tan" to encourage you to be open and calm.

A LITTLE RABBIT LOOKS FOR MUM

My dear little rabbit, when you are eleven months old, it is the first time that the World Expo is to be held in Germany. Dad and Mum are very busy. Most of the time your dad is in China – Mum has to stay in Germany. With no other way, Mum said to your dad, "Old rabbit, you should take the little rabbit back to China but in a basket". Before you boarded the airplane, your father bought a child's folding chair, not a basket, and took you on the plane.

It was the first that you left me, flying from one side of the earth to the other. With two transfers, and flying for over twenty hours, so you could meet your grandparents, auntie, and cousins who live in Wuhan China. Now you've gone for almost two months. I am still busy with work, overwhelmed by missing you. I begged your dad, "Please, bring our son back. I would rather work less, and earn less, but have him".

When you arrived, I saw you in the baggage claim area. You were sitting on the luggage trolley, whilst your father waited for the luggage to emerge. You were beautiful to my eyes. I called out to the old rabbit to bring you out first, so I could hold you, but your father could not be bothered until he claimed all the luggage. As soon as you came out, I stretched my arms out to you, hoping you would excitedly jump into my hug. You looked at me as if I was a stranger, and you turned to your father crying. Dad laughed and put you on the floor. You stood there, still. There was no step towards me. Again, I opened my arms to welcome you. You hesitated a little before rushing back to your father, where you stood between his legs for protection. I wept inside.

Your home was waiting for you. Your toys ready to be played with. You were full of curiosity. Now bigger, you climbed onto your bed and jumped up and down many times.

You were clever not wanting to hurt yourself, when you wanted to climb off, you sat down and eased yourself to the edge of the bed, and automatically turned your body around, and slid down over the edge to the floor. As soon as your little feet hit the floor, they were off on another mission.

I lifted you onto the piano chair, and found that you could sit stably on the chair by yourself and plonk the piano. At the beginning you were a little hesitant. I was disappointed, after only two months and you couldn't play anymore. Two days later, to my delight, you played. This time, not like before, when you put all your body on the keyboard, you used different fingers to play the piano keys, gently and with concentration. You showed your mum an old fashion style. The only thing that had not changed was that you wanted an audience. Mum had to stay beside you, to applaud you, with the occasional, "Excellent, my boy. One more time please". Sometimes Mum was so excited she danced to accompany you. You would raise your head, and reward Mum with your smiles. When you had enough, I only needed to tilt the piano chair forward a little and you would slide your bottom down until your feet are on the floor.

As young as one and a bit, you started to mock adults. You mocked Mum's happiness with a funny face, patting the table, stool, hands etc. You learnt very quickly how to imitate Mum's dancing, you waved your hands in an exaggerated way, like you thought I did, you waved your bottom and stuck it out, and tease in other ways. But, my dear baby, a few days later, mum found that you could move your bum naturally with the music.

You also brought things to show Mum. Whilst Mum cooks in the kitchen, I heard your foot steps staggering as you dragged something for me to see. There was always a big toy in your arms, which made your walking unstable – you delight in showing me. There was one time I hid behind the wardrobe in the bedroom. After looking for me, you went to the kitchen, then the bedroom, but you didn't find Mum. You turned around and walked in the dark bathroom, where you burst into tears. When I rushed to the bathroom, sobbing, I picked you up, "Little rabbit, rabbit, Mum's here". My dear son, when I felt your need of me, I felt that you had returned. You are still that little rabbit who came out of Mum's belly.

LIGHT FESTIVAL IN
KINDERGARTEN

Because Mum got cancer, your grandparents came to Germany. They took care of you. They loved you. They developed routines for you. Grandpa's job was to take and collect you from kindergarten. But your grandpa only knew a few German words. Many times when your grandpa picked up not only his grandson, but also numerous notes with all kinds of instructions. Such as, "Dear Ms. Huang, Tantan need nappies; Dear Ms. Huang, Tantan is allergic to today's vegetables". There was one day, your grandpa took another note back. It was a letter that Grandpa could not understand. I read the message and it informed us of The Light Festival at school.

On that day, I had some important work to do. Before I left home, I grabbed the note and read it again, and then allocated work to your grandparents. "Grandma, can you please fry a box of shrimp slices, a box of spring rolls; they need to be kept warm. This afternoon at 4.00 pm, when you pick up Tantan, take them, they need to be hot; Grandpa, can I trouble you to take this note and go to the American shop, which is on the road corner and buy a lantern for Tantan, better not be over 10 Marks". As I left home, I heard my parent's laughing, "10 Marks is just 40 RMB. In China, for the festival you spend much more than that".

In the afternoon at 4.15 pm, Mom hurried to the kindergarten. On the kindergarten walls were pinned golden-yellow-dark red leaves, shrubs or dried branches with snowflakes. I was surprised when one of your teachers removed the decorations of summer's green, and replaced them with autumn clothes. But Mom had little time to appreciate the decorations. She had to greet the other children's parents, who Mom knew, as well as Tantan's little friends.

It was busy in the kindergarten, with activity everywhere. When Mom got to your classroom, you burst into the dining room calling, "Mum, Mum", whilst holding a big shrimp flake in front of my eyes for me to appreciate. It was a banquet. But the shrimp flakes, and spring rolls were all gone when I got there. Grandpa had followed you out of the dining room. My father was so proud of you, and took me in the big playroom. "Look at this", as he pointed a colourful pole with electric lights. "And here", grandpa took out a folded lantern cover, I saw more than the lantern cover, all in the same shape but with different colours, a mix of red, blue …. A young teacher came over and pointed to the lantern cover with Tantan's name. She said with a warm smile "Ms. Mei, the lantern cover chose by Tantan is all green. He only wants green, green and more green. This meant that it was an all green lantern." I looked at the lantern cover you chose. You chose a green flower, and mountain of green. I loved it. You didn't chose rich colours, like other children. Your choice made was unique, and was a life colour. You could have chosen a different tone. I was very happy about it.

The young teacher did not appreciate it like I did. She said, "Ms. Mei, you can help yourself to a plate of food if you like. The shrimp flakes that Tantan bought here were so tasty. They went very quickly. It's a pity that you didn't get any of yours." I looked at the table but still saw that there were all kinds of dishes; there were salads, fried meatballs, German cold noodles, with different desserts, as well as fruits. One plate that tantalised my palate was Arabic rice. It was in a large iron pan about 0.5 metre in diameter, 10cm deep. It was full of the rice. On top, there was a layer of almonds and pine nuts, toasted chicken legs – it was delicious. Every time I saw this dish, I wanted to eat it. I asked who made it, and found out it was Tantan's little friend, Thyna's, mother. This made sense as Thyna's mother wore a headscarf and was Muslim. I chatted with her are asked her for the recipe. Thyna's mother told me that she came from Syria. She said many Arabic countries enjoy this rice, and is usually only made for special days or celebrations; with the almond and pine nuts, it is expensive. I thought of the spring rolls and shrimp flakes that I organised. They are nice, but cheap. I felt a bit embarrassed. But Grandpa confirmed that it was the spring rolls and shrimp flakes that were the most popular and the fastest to be eaten.

I enquired what the lantern festival's history was, to the same young teacher. She told me, "In ancient times, there was a wealthy person, named St. Martin. He was very kind, and often gave his own coat to the poor when the snow came. Then, the poor people chose him to be the bishop. In order to memorialise him, the German people made 11th November of each year the Lantern Festival."

After the food was cleared away, the teachers, with children, lined up. Each child held a lantern. We all walked around the kindergarten, led by the young teacher, where we sung, *"Lantern, Lantern Sonne Mond und Sterne! Brenne auf mein Licht, brenne auf mein Licht, aber nur meine Liebe Laterne nicht"*. I followed with my lantern; stars blinking in the sky, my lantern blinking on the earth…

A few days later, I took Tantan to visit a friend of ours. My friend's daughter was five. Tantan and I sung the 'Lantern song' again. We asked the little girl if she could sing the song with us. She shook her head to indicate, "No". I was surprised, and asked her, "Have you not celebrated the lantern festival at your school?" "Yes, I have", she said "but we sing 'lantern, lantern, sun, moon, and star". So we learnt that there are many different versions for the lantern festival.

IS LIFE HEAVY?

Every morning, when Tantan opened his eyes, his words always were, "Mum, I love you".

Did he feel lonely and unsettled because I went out dancing for two nights?

Another time, Tantan said, "In China, one morning, I said to Dad, I want to see Mum... But Dad would not take me. I was so sad. I missed you Mum for a long time. Mum, I love you... I love Dad as well".

Tantan was brushing his teeth. He was very willful, and wanted to have a lot of tooth paste. I did not permit it. He cried again. He was sensitive now, and cried a lot when he was with me. I was firm with him and said, "Tantan, if you cry again, I will send you back to China, to your dad. When Dad goes to his business, he won't take care of you. You will have to go to Grandma". Again he cried as he shook his head, "No, no, Mum, I want to be with you".

In these two months, he finally understood that it is only me who takes him to kindergarten every day. That it is me who picks him afterwards to bring him home. He loved his dad, but he did not realise that his dad will not accompany him very much.

When I had to tell him, "That dad is in China, very far away", Tantan would say, "Yes, I feel sad".

Two days ago, I had to tell him again, "Tantan, Dad is in China, how about we find another dad? You could have one dad in China, one dad in Germany".

"No" he quickly burst out, "no, no".

Little kids know a lot in their heart.

I asked Tantan, "Is it good for two people to be together? Or is it better for three people to be together?" Tantan said, "Two people together is good". So I asked again, "So just us two? You don't want Dad?" He shook his head and said, "No, Dad does not treat you good".

This broke my heart. Even he knew that his dad treated me badly.

I asked him mechanically, "So, who treats Mum well?"

"Jim!" Tantan answered.

Yesterday was a rainy day. Tantan asked, "Mum... do people live in the sky crying?" And last Friday I picked him up from kindergarten and we went to the library. On the way Tantan stared at my feet, "Mum, you have new shoes". I was surprised by his observation. His observations are much better than mine.

Sometimes when I went to pick him up from kindergarten, he would say to me in a little voice, "You are the last mummy here". Actually, I was not the last mummy. I was surprised he was not like this before. In the past he wanted me to come later so he could play until the kindergarten was about to close its door. He did not care if I was the last parent, or if he had to been taken out by the carer to wait for me at the gate. He would be still singing, and full of joy. It was now that he started to feel insecure.

Because he is young and with other children he spoke more and more German.

Yesterday, after being in the supermarket, Tantan debated with me, "Do you think what you choose is what I like? I don't like all the things you bought". My son had moved from being a little cutie, to one who was more often angry and wanting to fight with me. When I shopped for food, I did so with nutrition in mind. But he wanted unhealthy food. When he was younger, he liked what I bought. Now he fought with me. I really needed to balance myself. One time though, when we came out of the supermarket, with me carrying two heavy shopping bags, he silently lagged behind. Suddenly, he caught up with me, "Mum, let me help, give me one bag". The bag was really too heavy for him, so I took out the washing powder and softener, then gave him the bag.

I CARRY ON

Another motivation for me to remain alive was that I did not want my young boy to have no mother. This was the strongest motivation. I took my son back to China to complete his primary school, which enriched his Chinese heritage and rooted Chinese culture into him. I bought him back to Germany, as I also wanted him to have that in his life. I sent him to the same high school which Einstein attended for a time. He has almost graduated now. Sometime life is like an exam.

I have a home in Beijing, and one in Berlin; I work like a migratory bird.

I have organised many art exhibitions, published over ten painting albums, and organised over a hundred concerts. I wrote two monographs, in both languages, and published two novels. There have been sixteen Chinese – Germany youth festivals, with many thousands of people attending (CCTV broadcasted twice, German TV broadcasted three times).

I endured and survived advanced cancer, in the same year as my animal totem. Fate made me a single mother. Now, a decade later, I think that I have passed all life's examinations.

However, this not the final exam. There will be more examinations. This is only a 'mid-term' that I have handed in. It is hard to say if I am satisfied with this exam paper. But I am very clear, in that I have two countries for the rest of my life. I love both China and Germany. I have started to walk around Germany's father river – the Rhine River, and I started to walk around China's mother river – The Yellow River. I hope I could get double nutrition from these two rivers, so that I can hand out a better final life-exam paper.

I am grateful that I could write this book. It was a necessary requirement for my physical and emotional recovery. I am delighted that this book of my life struggles has travelled everywhere. But I am even happier for the acknowledgement and feedback that I have received, and that it has helped people.

Splendid spread over the sky

The life island are still wide, broad, deep and further

POSTSCRIPT:
LOOK FOR HOPE IN DESPAIR

Five years ago, I published a thin autobiographical novel, *The right to speak in marriage*. When writing my second novel, a friend from the publishing industry, encouraged me to face life – that is, to write it in the first person. I was timid but he said by doing so I would encourage more readers to look for hope in despair. Now, this book, *Reflections, Love Until Death* (the original name was called *Love Until Death*) appears in front of you, as a reflection of my life with cancer, and destructive relationships.

When I started the writing, I was only going to give some aspects of my life, as I was reticent. However, in the process of writing many of my friends supported and encouraged me to put more of me into the book. When I gave the partial manuscript, in German, to Deeter, a friend of mine, to ask him if he would help me edit the German text – and to ask him if he could help me contact a German publisher, almost immediately, he phoned me, and enthusiastically shouted, "My God, I read your manuscript, it is so touching. You have so much to offer readers. I have known you for many years, and I never knew these things about you. We have to meet immediately".

Deeter and his partner are researchers at the *German Natural Science Institute*. Over the past ten years, we have met at the dance hall in Berlin. I thought that they had a basic understanding of my experiences, but they did not. I seldom talk of my experiences, even to my colleagues. Deeter urged me to let him show the draft (German translation) to the French Artist, colour specialty Ms. Juliet, and Ms. Paula, who is a highly qualified artist, professor of Art Faculty of Naples University, and Vice Chairman of the German Federal Accordion, Ms. Heidi, who obtained the highest honour – Cross Medal of the Federal Republic of Germany.

I felt that I could not be totally free in my writing but they convinced me to open my heart. I hope to get your feedback.

I gave the Chinese version, firstly to my director, Mr. Zehou Li. I also sent it to the famous history and art commentator Ms Yi Ying. Representative of Senior Female Artist Ms Yunlan He. My university classmate, Mrs. Xinzhong Xu who is a professor of Beijing Guanghua Management College. I respect these people immensely.

In the year 2017, my old tutor Mr. Zehou Li is almost eighty-eight year's old. He recently returned to Beijing from America. Gratefully, he took the time to read my manuscript. I cherish this valuable time between us.

The feedback from these friends came back quickly. On the one hand, their comments brought tears to my eyes; on the other, their literature comments made me smile from the heart. I am sincerely grateful to all of them.

Once, my good friend, Melts and I, discussed Hermann Hesse, she recommend a few poems of his to me. I was so taken with them that I translated one into Chinese.

The Phase of Life by Herman Hess (my direct translation)

> All flowers finally fallen
> Youth replaced by elders
> However, each phase of life bloomed
> Each wisdom bloomed
> Each trait bloomed
> But they only belongs to its phase
> No need to be immortal
> This heart, faced each call of life
> It prepared to say good-bye
> Restart the sail
> In order to keep the passion
> No sadness
> Pass on the link to others
> Magician will be at each beginning
> Offer protection and help
> We should be happy to run from one space to another
> Not care too much to anywhere like to your hometown
> Spirit of exploring the world doesn't want to restrict or limit us
> It only want to improve us, step by step
> We just return to the hometown
> Form a close group
> We are warned
> Only people who prepared to get back to the new journey
> Can get rid of lazy habit
> The time of death may come
> It built a new space for us
> But the calling from life would never stop
> Good-bye! This heart, to keep health and say good-bye!

When I left Jim, I had nothing but an oil painting (the name of this painting is *"Lotus flower and Water Lily"*). In the painting, the front-on view was of a woman wearing the traditional Xiang Silk blue cheongsam, where she sits gracefully on a chair. Her dignified face is looking straight out of the painting at the viewers. At the bottom of the painting, lotus flowers emerge from mud and are lively in their bloom.

A second woman stands behind, she is naked, except for a red scarf around her hair. She clearly is a contrast to the woman who wears the blue cheongsam and white headwear. The second woman stands among water lilies.

At the corner of this oil painting, there is the signature of the artist, Yulong Han, 1996. Yulong Han is a well-known student of the *China Central Art University*. He lives in France.

This painting depicts, that irrespective, of wearing a cheongsam or of being naked, even when suffering cancer, the spirit is always there.

Oil painting by Yulong Han (80cm x 120cm). Both ladies in the picture are me. This picture was hung on the wall of my residence in Berlin for over twenty years

Life needs to be shared, especially when special circumstances occur.

AUTHOR'S NOTE

My thanks to the TianDi Publisher, with special thanks to my chief Editor, Mr. Wanwen Zhang, and Duty Editor, Ms. Suran Chen.

When our publishing contract was signed, they set up the Wechat (social media) edit group named, 'Teacher Mei Huang book publishing group'. In this group we continually discussed the manuscript and the edit, the final draft, how to promote it, the name of the book, chapter titles, chapter abstract, preface, cover .... The editors read my manuscript repeatedly. I have now published over ten monographs, translated books, and painting albums, which were edited by me. But this is the first time I had so much consultation with the publisher. Sometime I felt annoyed, but generally, it was very good.

Also, deep thanks to my friend Haizhen, who did her best to convince me to write this book. She also assisted with much and wisdom, she contribute ideas to this book

2017 – 2018 at Beijing and Berlin

Click here to see what Mei was up to when this book was going to press

https://youtu.be/oRRakXJUX6Q

If you enjoyed *Reflections, Love Until Death*, be sure to see book catalogue (and especially our books of Chinese heritage) on our website.

Published by Heartspace Publications, Australia

www.heartspacepublications.com

pat@heartspacepublications.com

Tel; +61 0450260348

www.ingramcontent.com/pod-product-compliance
Lightning Source LLC
Chambersburg PA
CBHW070251010526
44107CB00056B/2425